Hearing All Voices

Hearing All Voices

Culturally Responsive
Coaching in Early Childhood

Jill McFarren Avilés and Erika Amadee Flores

 Redleaf Press®
www.redleafpress.org
800-423-8309

Published by Redleaf Press
10 Yorkton Court
St. Paul, MN 55117
www.redleafpress.org

First edition 2021
Cover design by Renee Hammes
Cover illustrations by AdobeStock.com/Cienpies Design and AdobeStock.com/Klavdiya Krinichnaya
Interior design by Douglas Schmitz
Typeset in Minion Pro
Printed in the United States of America
28 27 26 25 24 23 22 21   1 2 3 4 5 6 7 8

Library of Congress Cataloging-in-Publication Data
Names: Avilés, Jill McFarren, author. | Flores, Erika Amadee, author.
Title: Hearing all voices : culturally responsive coaching in early childhood / Jill McFarren Avilés and Erika Amadee Flores.
Description: First. | St. Paul, MN : Redleaf Press, 2021. | Includes bibliographical references and index. | Summary: "Hearing All Voices offers a culturally responsive framework that supports educators in understanding the importance of equity in their interactions with children and families. The framework focuses on implementing practical strategies that can help increase equity in early education through day-to-day interactions. Written as a guidebook to support early childhood coaches to get inspiration, knowledge, and tools as they guide teachers from diverse backgrounds in early childhood settings. This book weaves together the latest in the science of change, brain development, adult learning, and practical 'how-to' to transfer this into practice"— Provided by publisher.
Identifiers: LCCN 2021027730 (print) | LCCN 2021027731 (ebook) | ISBN 9781605547527 (paperback) | ISBN 9781605547534 (ebook)
Subjects: LCSH: Early childhood education--Social aspects. | Early childhood teachers—Training of. | Culturally relevant pedagogy. | Parent-teacher relationships.
Classification: LCC LB1139.23 .A85 2021 (print) | LCC LB1139.23 (ebook) | DDC 372.21--dc23
LC record available at https://lccn.loc.gov/2021027730
LC ebook record available at https://lccn.loc.gov/2021027731

Printed on acid-free paper

In memory of my parents, who taught me the power
of listening, and to my husband and children for their
unwavering encouragement and support to follow my dreams.

—Jill

To my beloved parents, and to all the amazing early
childhood professionals who are fueled with passion
to make a positive impact in the lives of young children.
May your voices always be heard.

—Erika

Contents

Foreword

Adriana is a little teary this morning. She had a difficult time saying goodbye to her mama at drop-off. She is new to this multicultural Head Start room of eighteen- to twenty-four-month-old toddlers that I have the joy of working with this year. Her tender feelings have been apparent to all of us this past week as she adjusts to the strange, new space, all of the unfamiliar people, and the sounds of the adults speaking languages different from those her family uses. A teacher gently guides Adriana to the breakfast table to join the group. Fellow student Ester seems to know what will help. She eagerly leaves her seat and goes to the shelf to find Adriana's family photo and brings it to her. Adriana gratefully accepts, and her teary face seems to relax a little bit.

After breakfast the two children play next to each other at the sand table, where Adriana reciprocates Ester's earlier helpfulness and holds out a cup for Ester to use. Ester smiles and begins to fill the cup; then she turns and hands it back to Adriana. Passing the cup back and forth becomes a game of "we help each other," which the children happily play over and over again.

The next day the children are playing in the gym, where there is an empty row of cubbies up against the wall. Maya, who has already had her second birthday, is skillfully climbing in and out of the cubbies when Ester comes over to join her. Maya sees that Ester is struggling to pull herself up and thoughtfully reaches out to offer Ester a hand. Ester readily accepts this small support. The children join together side by side in the cubbies, peeking around the dividers and celebrating with giggles when they see each other's smiling faces.

On another day, I notice Anthony keenly focused on playing with a shape sorter, struggling yet determined to fit wooden blocks into the matching spaces of the larger block. Ester sees his difficulty and comes over to help. She takes a block from his hand and demonstrates what to do. Anthony screeches, "No, no!" Ester keeps insisting he do it her way, despite his clear, strong desire to figure this task out for himself. Ester finally gets the message and leaves him to his work.

I collect many small stories like these of children's natural skills and dispositions for empathy, compassion, belonging, and fairness. These moments give me hope for humans, as it seems clear—and research suggests—that young children are born with a strong desire to know, understand, and help others in ways that build equitable relationships.

I am starting the foreword of this book about culturally responsive coaching with these stories because I believe the children's ideas and actions in these moments can inspire adults to draw on our own compassionate nature in our work as culturally responsive coaches. The children's skills and dispositions in these stories also closely reflect the wisdom offered by the authors, Jill McFarren Avilés and Erika Amadee Flores, for the work of coaches in this beautiful book. The reflective questions that follow give you a taste of the ideas the authors offer in the book.

Can you identify the interactions in these observations of children that you might draw upon as a culturally responsive coach? Here are some possibilities:

- Ester understands that Adriana needs comfort in this strange, new place. How does your work as a coach acknowledge, celebrate, and center the culture of the people you work with?

- Adriana wants to show how she appreciated Ester's compassion by passing the cup of sand back and forth. How do you practice reciprocity in your work as a coach, joining together with the people you coach and sharing ideas, helping, and learning from each other?

- Maya closely observes and identifies Ester's struggle to climb and responds with the small support Ester needs to complete her goal. Their connection is strengthened as they share the joy of finding each other in the cubby spaces together. How can you closely observe and come to understand what will be useful for the people you coach to find their own way? How willing are you to accept help in your work as a coach? How do you feel when what you offer makes a difference? How do you share the joy of the connection you have made from the work you have done together?

- Anthony has clear ideas about what he is doing and how he wants to do it. Even though Ester's desire to help is admirable, she insistently tries to show him the way even when he is adamant that he wants to do it his own way. How do you ensure that your coaching supports people to do things that they feel strongly about in ways that support their growth rather than taking over for them?

- In all of these stories, even the spicy moments between Anthony and Ester, belonging, compassion, fairness, and equitable relationships are the essence of the children's focus. How do you put these important values at the center of your work as a coach?

The book is about cultivating equitable relationships, focusing on hearing and illuminating the voices of people whose voices are marginalized in the early childhood profession. The authors include a multitude of meaningful ways to help you and those you coach to identify, connect, and celebrate your own rich culture and values, while negotiating the reality of the white dominant culture of the profession. They put authentic, respectful relationships front and center in all of their approaches. The book offers rich descriptions and celebrations of different cultural values and experiences. The stories of the authors' own experiences of not fitting in and their love of being immersed in different cultural perspectives are powerful. They both describe their feelings of being invisible and not knowing how they fit in when they have been in a culture different from their own. They use their own life journeys, as well as their work as coaches in a variety of settings, to share ideas for getting to know your own culture and the culture of the people you mentor and to show how this affects the coaching process. Their life stories reflect why culturally responsive coaching is so necessary for negotiating the painful difficulties but also for engaging with joy and pride. As I read this manuscript, I often found I could picture myself in the coaching moments they describe.

In this era of standardization based in white supremacy and the push to prove that what we do with children has the "desired learning outcomes," more and more coaches are being hired and trained to help educators achieve these results. This book will be particularly useful for coaches who are working in these settings with tools that require you to gather data and meet an abundance of the standardized requirements, assessments, and quality rating scales that permeate our white-dominated profession. Often these tools are connected to funding, so it is serious business for teachers and providers to meet these demands. The authors approach this work with attention to building relationships and the culture and values of the people they are coaching. They desire to cultivate a process of inquiry that promotes rethinking how the definition of quality could look using a diverse and equitable lens. They offer a paradigm shift surrounding who owns the knowledge, based on one's role, language, identity, and economic circumstances. They remind us to question who gets to define what quality early childhood education is. Who is asking the questions and determining the answers? Whose voices are missing? Who is being marginalized and harmed by our current definitions of quality, and how do we coach people to get there?

I was honored that Erika and Jill invited me to write the foreword to their important new book. I was also reluctant to write it. I am a white woman who has been in the early childhood field for a very long time, and my voice along with other white people's voices have dominated and created an early childhood profession that is centered in whiteness and promotes white supremacy. This fact has produced deep inequities, particularly for black and brown and non-English-speaking children and adults.

I have come to understand that it is time for me and other white people to step aside to make room for other voices and work to decenter whiteness and counter white supremacy in our profession. Agreeing to write this foreword, and again centering a white voice to begin this book, seemed contradictory. Yet I have come to understand that for women of color to openly name white supremacy can be unsafe. As a white woman, I don't have to be fearful of a response when I speak the importance of countering white supremacy and send an urgent call for equity. We want white people to read and use the ideas in this book. Unfortunately, people may still value white voices above others, so my intention as I write this foreword is to illuminate the voices that are often made invisible. I hope my endorsement will propel you to use this book, to join in the work to counter the inequities in our profession, and to uplift the marginalized voices of the people who make up the bulk of our workforce.

For me the visionary possibilities this book invites are this: when we seek, value, celebrate, and genuinely center the voices, experiences, and interpretations of quality from diverse communities, we might be able to counter the inequities and harm that our dominant white culture has enabled. I look forward to more stories from Erika and Jill as they continue their work to reimagine and make visible diverse and equitable approaches to quality early education that can benefit us all.

—Deb Curtis

Acknowledgments

Jill

Thank you to all the coaches and early childhood leaders who have shared their wisdom and commitment to set educators up for success, and to the early childhood educators who have trusted me to accompany their professional journey. You have affirmed the power of partnership and meaningful reflective practice in driving sustainable change. A special thank-you goes out to the Child Development Home (CDH) early childhood educators and Briya Public Charter School staff in Washington, DC, and the Early Head Start and Head Start educators and partners in Fairfax County, Virginia. Your relentless commitment to children's and families' learning and well-being, especially during the COVID-19 pandemic, is a heart-given gift that will positively impact their lives for years to come.

Thanks to Susan Goettl and Duan Shankle and the rest of the Fairfax County team for their uncanny understanding of the importance of responsiveness and system-level thinking. Your investment in early childhood and ongoing professional learning from an equity lens is laying the foundation for lifelong learning for all.

Thank you to Esperanza Estrada and Elena Ramirez for your wisdom as leaders and educators, and for your relentless drive in supporting family child care business owners to achieve their dreams. Our conversations affirmed that the content in this book was relevant and essential.

To Caroline Davis, Cindy Gonzales, and Maria Gallagher, who coined the English phrase "no binga banga" because they couldn't pronounce *no hay mal que por bien no venga*. You have been a constant reminder that "there is no wrong from which right does not come."

A special thank-you goes to Ana Hoover, who has been a constant lifeline for me from our childhood days in Bolivia and now is a wise and calm associate-partner who understands the true gift of time. Her deep understanding and expertise around inclusion and her unceasing pursuit to achieve her career goals are truly an inspiration.

To my coach, Carolyn Turner, who effortlessly mirrors the principles of meeting clients where they are, and whose reflective questions deepened an understanding of who I am and supported my journey as a coach and woman business owner. Her reminder to listen to my inner voice continuously guided me to go where there was energy.

To my colleagues and friends with whom I've worked internationally, thanks for exemplifying the importance of humility and listening to the voices of children and community leaders. Our stories may be different, but they all are equally important to hear.

Melissa York, our editor at Redleaf Press, thank you for your thoughtful questions and thorough editing of our book. Your keen ability to read our minds and understand what we meant to say helped us get our thoughts across so that they could be heard and be meaningful to others. Renee Hammes, thank you for your creativity, patience, and passion to make sure the cover design conveyed the messages of the book. Deb Curtis, thank you for your thought-provoking wisdom and passion to really see children, along with your encouragement and moral support to submit our manuscript to Redleaf Press.

And last, to Erika for the many rich conversations that prompted us to write this book together and for your unwavering drive to make this a better world today and in the future.

Erika

I want to thank my parents, Irma, Norma, Jena, Jesus, and Roberto, for their lifelong love and their dedication to providing the best life possible to all of their children. You are the foundations that supported me in writing this book. Thank you to all of my siblings for continuing to honor the cultural and linguistic heritage that our parents have cultivated in us.

I want to thank my husband, Mario, for his consistent support, love, and encouragement. Thank you for being with me during every step in the creation of this book!

Thank you to all of my clients who have allowed me to be part of their professional journey in the field of early childhood education. It is the cultural and linguistic diversity of each and every single organization, coach, teacher, director, administrator, child, and family I have supported throughout my professional life that inspired the ideas in this book.

Thank you to Amy Stephens Cubbage, Johana Cabeza, Rogelio Chapa, and Matthew Lawrence for being amazing early childhood professionals, leaders, coaches, and friends who walk the talk every day. Your work in the field inspired this book and my life every day!

A very special thank-you to Marcela Clark for believing in and empowering me. Thanks to you, this book was able to become reality.

Thank you to Redleaf Press for giving us the opportunity to have our voices heard. Especially thank you to Melissa York for truly understanding the contents of the book and helping distill the ideas to make the best impact possible in every word. Thank you to Renee Hammes for putting your heart and creativity into action in designing the cover of the book.

Thank you to Esperanza Estrada and Elena Ramirez for sharing your voices during the initial interviews we conducted as the contents of this book were being developed.

And a deep, warmest gratitude to Deb Curtis for being a mentor and supporter. You are the fairy godmother of this book!

Thank you, Jill, for cowriting this book with me. Creating this book together and offering it as a gift to the field of early childhood has been a wonderful journey.

Introduction

We are so happy you are here! This book is about you. It is about your coaching clients and the rich cultural heritage that is an integral part of who we are in early childhood. It is about the diverse young children and their families whom your program serves. By diverse, we are referring to the wide range of racial, linguistic, and cultural backgrounds we encounter, as well as the environmental settings, the educational background of educators, the ages of the children, and the differing needs of each family.

This book was written for you and for your clients, for the unique values, beliefs, and practices that you as a coach and each client you work with bring to the field of early childhood education. You have your own unique culture, and your clients have their own unique culture. Let us deepen our understanding about our cultures and use the strength that each one brings to grow our field of early childhood education and be of better and more equitable and responsive service to children, families, and society.

Coaching is one of the strongest tools available to improve the quality of early childhood education. We define *quality* in early childhood education as the ability to understand and connect with the child's essence and to support children's innate drives as they develop within their social and cultural context. We propose that culturally responsive coaching follows a parallel process. We know that by working one-on-one with clients, we are able as coaches to provide individualized support that can help them grow and provide better service to young children and their families.

This book was born after a series of conversations with our clients and colleagues in early childhood about our field and current coaching practices. We hope that as you read through this book, it provokes reflection and builds awareness of your cultural beliefs and practices and that of your clients, at both a systems or organizational level and a personal one. Our profession is culturally and linguistically rich, and it mirrors the diversity found in the United States and across the globe. When we celebrate this diversity with our clients, we set the stage to nurture our connection and our innate drive to learn and evolve together.

We realize that many of the current coaching practices put pressure at various levels to comply with assessments and standards in the name of improving the quality of early childhood. Many of these assessments do not take into consideration the cultural and linguistic backgrounds of the field. When we see each other as equals and value everyone's differences, we can move away from a cookie-cutter approach that is based on dominant values. These dominant practices may have the best intentions, but because they are not responsive to diversity, they end up stifling learning and development because of the heavy emphasis on checking the box to comply.

In our current societal paradigm, using data to quantify any intervention has taken a huge priority. We know that as a coach, you likely face pressure to support your clients (teachers, directors, educators, and so forth) to increase their effectiveness in assessed areas in a specific amount of time. Though this push may have incredibly positive and helpful goals, it may also be putting unnecessary stress on coaching and early childhood overall. This added strain may cause coaches and educators to lose sight of the high-level view of why and what they are doing. Coaching models become focused on showing quantifiable outcomes related to the program, sometimes striving for just a few more points on an assessment tool or simply checking off for compliance. And sometimes this results in the individual who is being coached, your client, getting lost in the process.

We ask: Can coaching to the tests truly bring long-term sustainable change? Do the tools used to assess quality take into account the diverse makeup of our field? Is the data used to show compliance, or does it serve as a tool for reflection and understanding? What would be possible if we took the time to connect to the culture of our clients to deepen our relationships and to be truly attuned to our clients' needs?

It takes a combination of art and science to find the right balance between achieving set goals while at the same time making sustainable change in your clients' professional development and their potential to positively impact the field of early childhood education. If you really want to help in the field of early childhood, change needs to be meaningful, sustainable, and client-driven, based on a client's own goals for growth as a professional. It must include change in yourself as a coach, in your client, and at the organizational level. Sustainable change means that the knowledge and competencies built through the coaching relationship continue to grow. Whatever the client has learned or gained during the coaching relationship has become a new practice that will last a long time, not dependent on or restricted to what one person says.

The early childhood field is richly diverse in terms of culture, educational backgrounds, settings, and institutional goals. Thus, there is a sharpening focus on cultural responsiveness and equity in early childhood to ensure that diversity is an asset and equity is achieved. As a coach, you may be searching for tools and support to mirror culturally responsive and relationship-based practices. You may have the understanding that early childhood professionals need to make sustainable change while respecting diversity and fostering equity. Diversity and inclusivity are strengths, and they must be upheld if we are to address the inequalities that inhibit both young and adult learners from achieving their full potential. We embrace this philosophy as a fundamental principle in supporting educators in their ongoing professional learning process. It is through the culturally responsive coaching process that educators have the opportunity to feel heard as individuals and break down the barriers to learning they face, no matter their background, race, language, gender identity, anatomical sex, gender expression, or sexual orientation.

This book is a guide that offers tools to help you be much more responsive to your coaching clients' culture. Our goal is to help increase cultural responsiveness so that we can build equity and celebrate the uniqueness of individuals in our society. Our book is about making visible and celebrating our human connections and hearing and learning from all voices. Thus we understand ourselves and value each other as equals to ultimately support children in reaching their optimal potential!

We want to model how to be self-reflective about one's professional practice, developing a specific plan to reach meaningful, authentic goals. This practice focuses on discovering our strengths and the little steps that we take to get to that goal, implementing it, being patient and understanding of ourselves, and seeing the results. We support the client in learning how to go through a similar process with themselves even when they do not have a coach available.

We developed our culturally responsive coaching framework from our own experience, and it is supported by research as well. Our framework focuses on implementing practical strategies to increase equity in early education through day-to-day interactions, supporting educators to understand the importance of equity in their interactions with children and families.

After working in the field of early childhood education extensively, wearing multiple hats, we concluded that we must ensure educators' perspectives are holistic, culturally responsive, and strength-based, three necessary ingredients to enhance the lives of young children and their families and contribute to equity in early childhood settings. We are writing this guidebook to support you as an early childhood coach to get inspiration, knowledge, and tools to help you as you guide your clients from diverse backgrounds in early childhood settings. This book weaves together the latest in the science of change, brain development, and adult learning, and offers practical "how to" ideas to transfer this information into practice.

Our approach is to engage in a conversation with you and take an inclusive and equity-focused view of your role as a catalyst for change. The responsive strategies can be implemented in center-based and home-based early childhood settings. We present case studies from our experience and others' in working with a diversity of educators, highlighting the importance of taking a holistic, culturally responsive, strength-based approach and connecting work to real life. This guidebook is intended to be a pleasant reading experience for you, with space for your reflections and rich content to bring inspiration to your work as a coach in the field of early childhood education.

The conversations, reflective questions, and strategies presented in this book aim to bridge the voices of the educators who influence the lives of children and families with the sociocultural environment we live in, which is ever evolving. We hope that it invites you to reflect on your experiences and open yourself to possibly some difficult conversations about what it means to be culturally responsive. The ultimate goal is to make a difference in the lives of children and their families in an equitable way while listening to everyone's voices.

Our Story

We, the authors, first met one day in a little restaurant in a small town together with other colleagues over dinner. With a delicious glass of wine, we chatted in Spanish, a language we naturally fall back on, about early childhood and the work we do in the field. We found a lot of interconnectedness between our work as well as our philosophy and values in the field. Over the years, we've discussed our reflections, coaching practices, and what was working for us and our clients. After presenting together at several conferences, we decided to create this book in response to the current cultural climate and the needs in our field of early childhood education.

Erika's Story

My passion for early childhood education began from my own early experiences as a young child. I was born in Chicago, Illinois, to parents who had recently immigrated to the United States from Mexico. Since my birth, I have lived in a multicultural context and have felt the influence of other countries. When I was a young girl, we spoke Spanish at home and very little English. It wasn't until I began preschool that I actually started learning the English language. I loved my preschool experience, which was in a Head Start program. I was a lucky child, as my teachers were warm, loving, and welcoming to my family and to me. However, at that time there were not as many resources as today to support families who speak a language other than English. I remember that from early on there was something quite different about myself and my family compared to others. I realized that my family's culture was not part of the dominant or mainstream culture.

As I grew up, there was very little representation of my family's heritage and history. I remember at some point even feeling embarrassed to speak Spanish or to say that my family was from Mexico. The dominant society was sending the message that diversity was not valued. This was quite unfortunate. Then, when I was eleven years old, my mom, my siblings, and I moved back to Mexico. It was a very difficult change because I had already put down strong roots in my social identity as an American and had to learn a mainstream culture for a second time.

What a different world I found when I moved to Zacatecas, Mexico! To my surprise, I loved it. The town was rich in art, cultural events, and colorful traditions. I was able to immerse myself in fine arts, an opportunity I had not been given as a young child growing up in a low-income family in the United States. In Mexico at that time there were many free programs to help children learn about the arts and other cultural interests. I was able to embrace my family's Mexican cultural heritage while still maintaining my social identity as an American. At around that time my interest in human development also blossomed. By age thirteen, I realized that I wanted to dedicate myself to helping improve others' lives. I was pretty sure I would pursue psychology, as I had visited a counselor for support as my family and I went through difficult life circumstances.

I truly admired the counselor's work and the positive impact she'd had on my family. I have clear memories of times when I was not properly supported as a bicultural child as I continued traveling across the border between the United States and Mexico during my formative years. Then and now I think of the countless other children going through the same experience, whose families have immigrated from every country in the world. I realized that I wanted to dedicate myself to a field in which I could help humans develop their potential and help prevent problems in society before they arose, and I discovered I could achieve that in early childhood education.

As the years passed, I was further immersed in different cultures. I became an exchange student in Budapest, Hungary, and then explored other nearby countries, over time becoming a seasoned world traveler. Consistently I've tried to take a nontouristic approach when I visit other countries to learn about other cultures. I really try to understand the different perspectives and the values that each culture brings. My love of cultures and my love for humanity fuels my passion in the field of early childhood education, and thus this book was born.

My professional journey took me to get a degree in psychology and later a master's degree in instructional leadership in early childhood education. Throughout the years, I've worn many hats in the field, supporting culturally and linguistically diverse programs as a teacher, researcher, trainer, coach, university instructor, consultant, presenter, and writer. During the time that I have worn all of these hats, I have always been seeking to find and implement the most innovative and impactful tools and approaches to help children and their families.

Then I decided to start my own company. I founded ChildrenFlow, an organization whose mission is to develop each child's unique being and deepen their interconnectedness with the world that surrounds them. ChildrenFlow fulfills its mission by providing impactful professional development products and services to early childhood initiatives to help build a better and happier world. I am committed to supporting initiatives in early childhood that respond to the rich variety of language and cultures in the United States. Not only does this colorful diversity reflect the children and families who enter our programs, but it is also a reflection of the teachers, assistants, directors, coaches, administrators, and all the way up to policy makers. My hope is that this book that Jill and I have written together will provoke further conversations and questions about advancing our field of early childhood education and building a more equitable world by being culturally and linguistically responsive.

Jill's Story

I am bicultural and bilingual, and I have not always felt that I fit in any one culture. My life began in Bolivia, the third of five children of American and Austrian missionary parents who valued equity, relationships, and respecting people for who they are. Influenced by my family and birthplace and the neighborhoods where I grew up, my multicultural environment gave me unique insight into seeing the world through different lenses. My early experiences in Bolivia, surrounded by a diverse community, learning when and how to use two languages, laid the foundation for my work in finding the unique gifts that we each have to offer. Every three to four years, we moved to the United States so we could immerse ourselves for a year in the US educational system. It was also an opportunity for my parents to share their story and raise awareness with sponsors about their work with communities and schools in Bolivia. I often wondered why the sponsors were so fascinated with something that was so mundane to me. Now I understand that we were looking at life through different lenses. After twenty-six years of service, my parents, who were in their mid-fifties, decided it was time to leave Bolivia and settle in the States. I was old enough to see them struggle to find jobs that were fulfilling and in which their unique skills of community mobilization in a very different cultural context would be valued. They also had to adjust to commuting long distances by car. Their persistence and belief in themselves and others were the cornerstone of their resilience!

At times it was not easy shifting between the different cultures, feeling confused about who I was and how I fit into this complex system of diverse beliefs and traditions. Although I didn't know it at the time, the experiences of being Bolivian and American prepared me to understand how our individual perspective on the world shapes our reality. I learned that sometimes we need to put a hold on who we are so we can stop and truly listen to other people's voices. It taught me that the filters we build from very early on limit our ability to be open and respect the ideas of others.

Over the course of my professional career, first as a Head Start teacher and then in a variety of roles working for US and international organizations, I met inspiring leaders whose passion was to serve others and foster compassion and resilience in those they led. The resilience came from affirming their strengths, building ownership through reflective questioning, and not being afraid to show their vulnerability or learn from their mistakes. These gifts they shared inspired me to build on and celebrate the strengths of others while fostering self-awareness and compassion. I also learned a great deal from children, especially in working closely with infants and toddlers. Their wonder at the world and with the simplest and most mundane experiences has taught me to feel awe at the beauty and wonder we often take for granted. Their innate drive to build relationships and to learn has become an essential part of what I strive to instill in others.

I started McFarren Avilés & Associates to partner with diverse organizations that are making an impact in the lives of children and their families. A major thrust of our work is fostering leadership and passion for lifelong learning in the Spanish-speaking early childhood community, especially with family child care educators. Engaging early childhood professionals in a language that is familiar and representative of their culture bridges a huge gap of knowledge and human connection. The energy, richness of the conversations, and overall well-being that we experience in the coaching and professional learning sessions is like no other. Synergy is created in a space where diverse voices are heard, respected, and lifted. I know that this positive energy is passed on to others through interactions with children and families. This book weaves these experiences together, along with Erika's, and aims to mirror the culturally responsive strategies that have been the backbone of our work. I hope the conversations permeating this book accompany you as a coach and offer the opportunity to reflect on your own journey as a servant leader striving to make lasting positive change.

How This Book Is Organized

We begin this guidebook with an overview of our philosophy around diversity, culture, and integrated approaches, which sets the stage for the rest of the chapters. The next chapter focuses on you as a coach, as the person you have the most control over. We highlight the importance of getting to know yourself, including what drives you and what your biases are, and how these qualities influence learning and connecting with others. We include strategies to practice self-compassion and being a servant leader. These are the foundational competencies needed to be a culturally responsive coach. This self-reflection mirrors the process you can then use with your clients to build a trusting relationship. The third chapter focuses on the client and how their experiences, values, language, culture, and professional goals can influence the coaching relationship. Understanding your client's culture at a deep level is essential for culturally responsive coaching. Chapter 4 looks into the culture of the diverse settings where your clients work. Understanding the setting will provide you with tools to be culturally responsive through your coaching. These first chapters set the stage to explore what coaching is about, the science and research behind strength-based coaching and how to do so in a culturally responsive way. Chapters 5 and onward emphasize the importance of a culturally responsive and equity-focused approach and share strategies and resources that you can use at different moments of the iterative coaching cycle, including the use of data from an equity and culturally responsive lens and how to support the resilience of your clients.

Throughout this guidebook, we use the word *client* instead of *coachee*. The primary reason for this is that it changes the perspective. The teacher or director or early childhood professional whom you are supporting as a coach is your client. And as with any client, we want to be very attuned to their specific needs and to be there to serve and support them as they reach their goals. This requires us to quiet our agenda and connect deeply with our client so we can support them in reaching their potential and their dreams in the field of early childhood education. We hope this book provides you with many insights, opportunities for reflection, and practical and actionable strategies to support equity and sustainable long-term change through culturally responsive coaching.

CHAPTER 1

Cultural Responsiveness for Sustainable Change

All of us in the academy and in the culture as a whole are called to renew
our minds if we are to transform educational institutions—and society—so that
the way we live, teach, and work can reflect our joy in cultural diversity, our
passion for justice, and our love of freedom.

—Bell Hooks

Voices from the Field: Erika

Walking through the city of Mumbai, I saw all the colorful shades of the rain-
bow. Bright pink, orange, blue, turquoise—all the colors that you can imagine!
Women walked around with gorgeous shawls; sounds of birds, waves, traffic,
and energetic pedestrians surrounded me as I walked by the famous arch of the
Gateway of India. The monument stands, strongly constructed, reflecting the
rays of the morning light as it testifies to the long history of these ancient lands.
The aromas of spices and the sea brought a dreamlike state to the moment. It was
my third day in India. Already I had visited several neighborhoods filled with tall
apartment buildings, small shops, children playing freely on the sidewalks, and
humongous statues of the Hindu god Ganesh that were heavily decorated with
flowers and other offerings. The residents were celebrating the festival of Ganesh
Chaturthi. I was told that the god Ganesh is the deva of intellect and wisdom,
and he removes all obstacles. Children's and families' faces were full of smiles and
light. I was delighted! Why is it that sometimes we have to visit a country that is
so different from our own to be able to be more aware of our culture and others?

   For years I had been attracted to India. This interest began when I started
learning yoga as a teenager in Mexico, including its philosophical roots and the

healing approaches of Ayurveda. Throughout the years, I had soaked up the country's long and ancient history. So when a friend invited me to accompany him on a visit to friends in India to study its culture, art, and philosophy, I did not hesitate.

In Ahmadabad we stayed with local friends in a suburb outside the city center composed of tall apartment buildings, clustered one after the other. The streets were full of life. Our hosts went above and beyond to provide us with the most enjoyable experiences. They cooked immense amounts of food, showed us the highlights of their city, and even organized a party at their apartment. Overwhelmed by so many stimuli from the day and the party, I went to my bedroom to try to get some rest, only to encounter several female party guests who walked into my bedroom to chat, fix their hair, and use the bathroom at the end of the room even as I was lying in the bed trying to nap. I was surprised! It seemed as though it was normal in their family to enter another woman's bedroom at any time without even knocking on the door. I laughed and rejoiced at the surprises that had arisen during this trip as I deepened my understanding of a completely unfamiliar culture.

Getting to know my hosts at a deeper level and developing a trusting relationship helped open doors so I could go beyond a merely touristic understanding of India. For example, one early morning I awoke to find one of my hosts reading the Bhagavad Gita. She translated a short part of this sacred Hindu scripture to me as we sipped tea together. I felt my soul uplifted. She also shared her values, how she raises her children, what would comprise a quality education for them, and how happy her arranged marriage has turned out for both her and her husband. Her culture fascinates me, and it opened up my heart to connect deeply with someone who seemed so different from me.

About two weeks into our stay, we visited Agra, where the Taj Mahal is located. It was evening. Soon I was to return to the United States. I escaped to our hotel's quiet swimming pool. There, as I swam peacefully, I reflected on my coaching clients and my work in early childhood education. Coaching is at the heart of the professional work I do. I thought about all the teachers, directors, coaches, young children, and families associated with the organizations that I support. Many of my clients are a reflection of our current global world—an intermingling of a variety of countries, languages, religions, values, and customs.

I thought deeply on how culture affects our actions and the decisions we make and how it can motivate us for growth and change. Could we make an impact in society by increasing our ability to respond to each and every person's history and culture? What positive impact could intentional cultural responsiveness have in coaching? Could coaching be more effective? How? I invite you to keep these questions in mind as we go through this chapter together.

Reflective Questions

- What does culture mean to you?

- As a coach, why would it be relevant for you to understand your client's culture?

- What do you know about your client's culture?

- What role could cultural responsiveness play in coaching?

- How do you show cultural responsiveness to your clients?

- Have you ever had challenges with a client because of cultural differences?

- Has culture ever played a role in resistance to change—yours or your client's?

In this chapter, we will explore what culture is and how cultural responsiveness is essential for human development and for the field of early childhood education. We willl discover what is meant by culture and cultural responsiveness, and see the role it plays in coaching. We will learn that everyone has culture, stemming from the beliefs, values, and practices that are unique to each person. We will also discuss how culturally responsive coaching can support equity and antidiscrimination in our society while showing respect for one another. One key focus of this chapter is an invitation to celebrate the diversity in early childhood and find ways through coaching to bring about sustainable change that positively impacts the lives of children and their families. This chapter lays the foundation for the rest of the book.

Culture

You have probably heard the word *culture* a lot. It is one of those buzzwords used frequently in many spheres. But what does *culture* really mean? How does one acquire culture? What role does it play in a person's life? Let us take a closer look at how a human develops culturally.

When you look into a newborn child's eyes, you see a deep and beautiful being within—their unique essence. That young human already has temperament traits and interests, and they will pass through many developmental stages in life. A person's essence interacts with the external environment to fully develop their potential; this interaction is how culture is formed. The environment that influences the child's development is composed of their family, caregivers, neighborhood, community, religious organization, city, state, and nation, and these factors add up to each person's own particular culture.

Culture is composed of the beliefs, values, and perspectives that influence our behavior and the decisions we make. The word *culture* has its roots in the Latin term *colere*, which means to tend, to cultivate, or to help grow. Historically, each community or group of individuals has evolved and developed culturally according to their values and needs. These values and needs are influenced by factors such as historical-social context, environment, aspirations, dreams, and challenges. Cultures are constantly growing and changing based on the specific needs of each era, community, or individual.

Often we are unaware of our own culture. Culture is like the ocean, and we are the fish swimming in it, unaware that we are surrounded by water. We all live in our own ocean, our own culture. Our culture is a strong reflection of who we are. It is also imprinted by our ancestors, their struggles, their victories, and their dreams. Culture influences us every day. Paying attention to our own culture allows for more intentionality. We can be more aware of what helps us move in the direction of our goals or what holds us back from advancing. Chapter 2 focuses on being more aware of your own culture.

Each of your clients has a long cultural heritage that affects their work in the field of early childhood education. Your client's culture affects the actions, motivations, and perspectives that drive their work in the field. We cannot ignore culture as an element that affects our coaching services and outcomes, but it would be a difficult task to know each and every culture. Each person's culture is unique—even within the same family unit. Therefore, to understand the culture of your client, you need to understand who they are as an individual. Chapter 3 takes a deeper look into how we can understand each client's culture.

Organizations and institutions also have their own culture, and this is certainly true in early childhood education. Initiatives to increase the quality of early care are influenced by specific values and perspectives. Our beliefs surrounding early childhood, our aspirations as a society, and our goals all influence the research, design, and implementation of programs. Many initiatives make efforts to root their decisions in science and research. However, even science cannot be fully free from culture's influence. The twentieth-century philosopher Thomas Kuhn deeply analyzed how science is influenced by the paradigms of its time. Our discoveries in science influence our culture, and our culture also influences science. They are interconnected.

Just think about the many approaches to early childhood education: constructivism, progressivism, Montessori, Reggio Emilia, Waldorf, and so on. Each arose from its historical and social context. Culture plays an active role in how we view and educate young children. In today's society in the United States, our philosophies surrounding the education of young children must evolve. Whose voices have been predominant in the current cultural values of early childhood programs? Whose voices are missing? Our society is ever becoming more culturally and linguistically diverse. Are these diverse voices being heard? Through coaching, how deeply are you listening to your client's culture?

We need to take culture into consideration if we are to fully support our clients. To do so, it is necessary to learn more deeply about our own culture, the program's culture, and the clients' culture to fully create a positive, lasting long-term change in the early years of young children.

Cultural Responsiveness

In early childhood education, we promote being responsive to a child's needs and interests. It is called *responsiveness* because we observe what the child is doing or needs in the moment and, based on that observation, we respond with an action that is attuned to that child at that time. To respond to someone's culture involves understanding the culture of that person and using that understanding to respond to their needs and aspirations.

It is important to remember that this understanding of culture is *not* based on stereotypes of particular nations or populations, but rather it depends on learning what has influenced a person's life and formed their habits, beliefs, aspirations, and values. Once we understand these cultural elements, we can then intentionally respond to truly support that person from a deep knowledge of who they are, the history they have lived, and where they want to go. Try to see the world from the client's perspective, listen, and put yourself in their shoes.

A specific competency related to cultural responsiveness is the ability to be interested in other cultures. It requires us to have curiosity. More specifically, to be culturally responsive to your clients requires being authentically interested in learning about their individual culture. Sometimes it may be uncomfortable to seek out information about different cultures because we don't want to offend others or seem silly. However, we invite you to be like a young child who is curious and asks questions without fear. In a similar way, you can also let your client know that you would like to learn about their culture and history to be able to better support them in your coaching relationship. You may also let them know that they can ask you questions about your own culture.

Even the most experienced world travelers who are constantly exposed to very unfamiliar cultures at times feel challenged to be open and learn about other ways of living. This is especially true when people from other cultures dress differently than you, speak a different language, or have a religion you know little about. It's okay if we sometimes feel uncomfortable because we don't want to insult someone or seem silly. It's okay to be vulnerable and not know everything. Developing a cultural responsiveness competency involves learning how to accept and embrace any vulnerability we feel in front of someone from a different culture.

Another essential element of culturally responsive competency is our ability to develop authentic relationships with people of diverse cultures. This means that we really get to know others and learn how to accept and respect their views, opinions, and perspectives. It doesn't mean that we must agree with everything we learn. We ourselves have our own particular culture, and we can share our values, dreams, and perspectives in a respectful way. However, our own culture should not be an impediment to developing a relationship in which we can collaborate harmoniously to reach common goals. Try to find ways to truly deepen client relationships based on mutual respect and acceptance of each other's culture. Dedicate time during your coaching sessions with your clients to learn deeply. Show interest and curiosity. Share your life and your own culture. Make connections between your own culture and life experiences.

Another element of cultural responsiveness is seeing the value that each culture offers and the social capital it adds to our world. By being open and curious and interested in your client's culture and sharing your own, you will be able to better support the client and therefore have a stronger impact in the lives of young children and their families.

Coaching

As human beings, we are all evolving at many levels: at a personal level as well as at the level of the family, community, society, nation, and global international community. As we grow, helpers support us in our personal goals as well as in the overall goals of society. These helpers are parents, teachers, mentors, therapists, counselors, shamans, priests, pastors, and on and on. How can you as a coach take the role of an authentic helper or servant leader by connecting at a deep level with your client, responding intentionally to their culture?

If we are to play the role of a coach, to be truly effective in supporting the client's growth and development, our work must stem from a full understanding of the client's essence and culture. Imagine trying to cultivate grapes for a wine like a French Syrah but caring for the plant as if it were a Spanish albariño. That grapevine will not flourish as well as it could have, had we given ourselves the opportunity to understand it at a deep level. We would get only sour wine. To help the Syrah truly flourish into a wine that has reached its fullest potential involves understanding the soil, light, and irrigation requirements and the exact time of harvest, among many other factors. In the same way, to help an early childhood professional produce their best, to create transformational growth, we must understand that individual deeply.

Currently there are many models for coaching in early childhood education. The culturally responsive strategies that this guidebook offers can be applied in diverse coaching models. It might be that you are coaching within a model that will help teachers implement a certain curriculum or improve their interactions or their environments. Whatever the end goal that was provided to you as a coach is relevant and important. However, we encourage you to take the time to fully understand your client's culture, including their own goals in the field of early childhood. We also encourage you to have open conversations about your client's ideas regarding the different tools and methodologies you are required to use through your specific coaching model and program goals. For example, are there discrepancies between the coaching program and your client's cultural perspectives regarding environments or certain adult-child interactions? What are their beliefs and experiences? Are the values of the program and your client aligned? Are there differences? If so, how can you support making your client's voice heard?

Cultural Responsiveness in Sustainable Change

We direct our efforts as coaches, directors, or pedagogical leaders of early childhood professionals to ensure we are providing the highest quality educational experiences. By quality we refer to the process of nurturing the inner drive to learn and connect in young children and giving appropriate support to their families. Through research and science, our field has worked hard to uncover the essential ingredients of quality education, based on our current understanding of human development. We also know that when our society changes, so do our goals and aims and so do the ways we define and support quality. But from our current paradigm, we understand that interactions are key for young children and that the environment plays a huge role in development.

Often our role as coach involves supporting the client to learn about these research-based principles and to find ways to implement them in their practice. We must seek a balance between science and the goals of a particular program and the culture, beliefs, and perspectives of the client we are supporting. We must ask whether we are there to fully support the professional growth of our client or simply trying to shape that person so they comply and implement what the current research standards are saying. Will the client have buy-in if we are simply trying to mold them to fit standards? Without buy-in, we may find ourselves with a client who just nods their head yes to everything we say but their actions realign with their beliefs and perspectives once we leave. We may see them incorporate some ideas but only temporarily.

When coaching falls into patterns of this sort, it takes a transactional approach, like when you go to a grocery store to buy apples. You grab your apples, go to the cashier, pay, get your receipt, and go home. This type of interaction can be a waste of our time, the client's time, and the organization's resources. Transactional coaching sessions in early childhood education generally start with what the program perceives as a "necessary change" in the client's performance. Then a plan is developed to address this "necessary change." Instruction and guidance are provided for making this change, taking away the client's ownership and agency in their professional growth and disregarding their goals and drives.

This may create a culture of blame and shame, which in turn can develop a sense of impotence and frustration in the client. Let's say that the client shows "change" in that perceived "need." How long do you think this client would sustain such change in their actual practice?

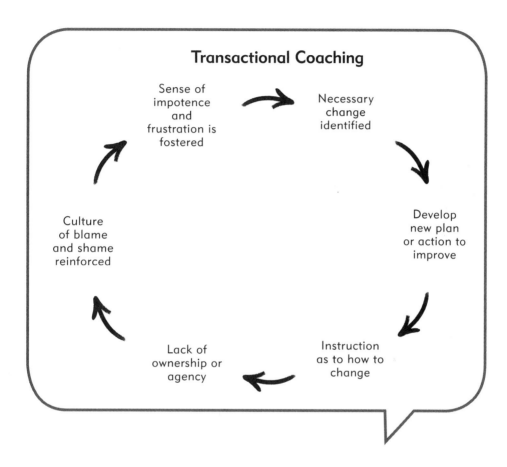

Cultural Responsiveness as a Transformational Coaching Tool

We want to challenge the perspective of transactional coaching for compliance and replace it with coaching to achieve culturally responsive change that is sustainable in the long term and fosters learning and connection in early childhood professionals. We already know that resources in our field are limited, so we must invest our resources in experiences that will truly lead to long-term improvement.

Through the culturally responsive approach to coaching, we establish and maintain trusting and positive relationships based on a deep knowledge of ourselves, including our own culture. We make efforts to know the client's culture deeply to build and sustain the relationship. Through coaching sessions, you support the client in identifying their own strengths, dreams, and values for their professional work. You help the client tap into their own professional vision and mission in supporting the learning and development of young children. Based on this, the client feels heard. The client's voice becomes the driving force in identifying areas where change is needed, and thus the client has ownership over the action items to achieve the goals. Through intentional coaching conversations, you build with your client a culture of self-reflection, learning, and investigation. You also empower the client's voice to be heard to build more equitable early childhood systems through grassroots efforts and help them be active agents in areas such as data and assessment. Throughout the process, you celebrate successes and also learn from mistakes.

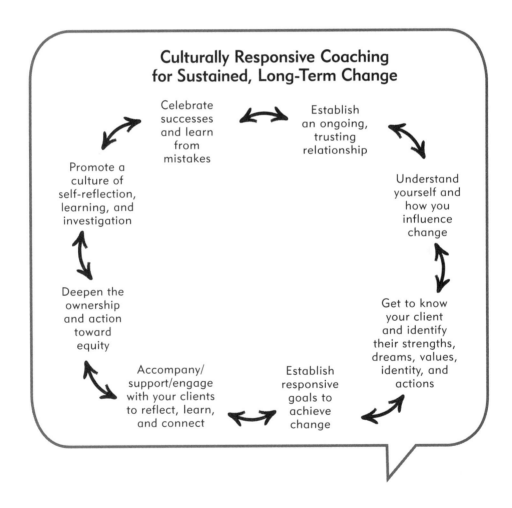

Culturally Responsive Coaching for Sustained, Long-Term Change

Celebrate successes and learn from mistakes

Establish an ongoing, trusting relationship

Understand yourself and how you influence change

Promote a culture of self-reflection, learning, and investigation

Deepen the ownership and action toward equity

Get to know your client and identify their strengths, dreams, values, identity, and actions

Accompany/ support/engage with your clients to reflect, learn, and connect

Establish responsive goals to achieve change

Culturally responsive coaching can also be a strong agent of change to support equity and antidiscrimination in our society. Let us take a look into both of these elements.

Equity

New cultural paradigms are always transforming society. Currently, we are pushing for a social transformation toward equity. The previous paradigm was focused on equality, in which every person was given the same. Equality has definitely helped advance our society; however, with the current events and knowledge of our society, we now believe promoting equity is critical. Equity involves understanding that each individual has specific needs that must be met to reach their goals. People do not need exactly the same thing (equality); rather, each individual needs more or less of certain types of support than others do (equity). To be equitable requires that we provide the support or tools each individual needs.

A common image used to show the difference between equality and equity imagines three children trying to reach an apple in a tree. The first is a very young child, the second is an older and taller child, and the third is the oldest and the tallest. In this example, the biggest child is tall enough to grab the apple, but the other two children are not able to do so. From an equality standpoint, each child would be given the same size box to stand on to try to reach an apple. With the same size box, the tallest child is still able to reach the apple and the midsized child is now able to get an apple too, but the shortest child is still not able to reach one. To be equitable, we instead provide different-sized boxes to each child so everyone can reach an apple. Some clients will need more time and more intense support from you, while others will need less frequent or shorter-lasting support. Some will need much more emotional support from you, while others will be ready to jump into very academic areas. Members of different cultural groups have different needs as well.

To be equitable coaches, we need to be very attuned to the actual needs of our clients, to meet them where they are in their development. When we understand their needs and base our coaching relationships on that, we are striving to demonstrate more equity. By doing so, we're hoping to move our society forward so that each individual has their needs met and can achieve their goals as early childhood educators. In chapter 4 we will explore specific strategies to use in your coaching to support equity by being culturally responsive to your clients.

Antidiscrimination work

Unfortunately, throughout the history of humanity and still today, racism and other forms of discrimination exist. Discrimination involves treating others unjustly based on race, gender, religion, age, nationality, sexual orientation, income, educational level, or other aspects of an individual. To truly advance as a society, we need to take an antidiscrimination and anti-racist stance. This involves taking an active role in identifying discriminatory biases in ourselves as well as in others. It also involves taking actions that will help prevent discrimination in any form. To be anti-discriminatory is not a passive task but an active one in which we need to speak out whenever we see discrimination taking place and take needed actions. In the following chapters, we will be taking a deeper look into specific strategies to support antidiscrimination through culturally responsive coaching strategies.

Relationships and Rapport

Coaching that springs from a strong relationship with a client can help initiate long-term change and growth. As human beings, we are social creatures. We live in groups. We have a need to be connected with other humans. This is an essential element of our development as a species. We have learned that when we work together, we can have our needs met and work toward goals that lead to our happiness and well-being.

As we have developed as a species, relationships have become an essential part of our learning and development. We have also developed a sense of which relationships are authentic and trustworthy. When we are in such a relationship, we feel comfortable to open up and to grow. However, if we are with another person who makes us uncomfortable, who does not understand us, or who brings their own agenda to impose on us, we may shut down. If we are to support early childhood professionals through coaching, it is essential to develop a strong and authentic relationship.

Rapport is one of the most fundamental aspects of building relationships. It involves truly seeing the world from the other person's perspective. It involves letting go of our own ideas, concepts, and perceptions to truly hear the voice of the other person and feel and see the world as they see it. When we do this, they feel understood and know they can trust you.

Understanding a client's culture helps us develop rapport at a deeper level. When we reflect on what a client has said, we're showing them that we are hearing them. By acknowledging that we understand their perspective, we can deepen the relationship. This can also help the client feel more comfortable and understood. Let us further explore aspects of building rapport—recognizing strengths, being present, and celebrating diversity—in more detail.

Being strength-based

Being strength-based involves focusing on the positive aspects of your client's work with young children. It highlights the cultural capital the client brings. We want to find very specific examples of the client's strengths, highlight them, communicate them, and use them as the base for further learning and development. When we start with the client's strengths, we can build on that foundation to help the client reach their professional goals.

Currently society tends to focus more on the negative. Frequently we point out what is wrong or look for what is missing. This approach may take clients to frustration, anxiousness, and higher stress levels. However, when we highlight strengths, we tap into the positive potential of our client and create an energy that fuels motivation for change and growth. Once a client starts reaching goals, we continue highlighting and celebrating these victories. By building on the positive, we can continue spiraling up in an everlasting cycle of learning and development to help the client reach their potential as an early childhood professional.

Being present

So much of the time we are focused on our own thoughts. This internal chatter can take a lot of space, preventing us from truly being present in the moment and being aware of the other amazing human being who is in front of us, our client.

Take a moment right now to be aware of your surroundings. Look intentionally through your eyes. Every three seconds, try to look at a different object intently. Look at its shape, colors, and details. Become aware of your body. Is it tense somewhere? How is your posture? How is your breathing? Bring your awareness to the sounds that surround you in the moment. Can you hear birds chirping or crickets making sounds? Be present in your moment.

Next time you are with your client, try to be similarly aware of the environment that surrounds you. Be attuned to your client. Notice the details. Look into their eyes and hear their voice, their tone, their message. Quiet your chattering mind. By doing so, you will be able to connect more deeply and truly learn about their culture and goals and how you can support them as a coach. Find ways to foster satisfaction each time you are with your client. What are their dreams? What are their fears? Connect. Be. Enjoy.

Celebrate diversity

Nature is endlessly diverse. Just look out your window and see the variety of trees, flowers, insects, birds, grasses, and of course human beings. Every living being brings its own contribution to life on planet Earth. Through this diversity comes the balance that helps life prevail.

Likewise, every culture offers wonderful and colorful elements to our experience as a human species. When we differ in opinions, beliefs, and experiences and we learn to hear and learn from each of these differences, we are challenged to push ourselves to our next level of cultural understanding. Each generation comes into the world to offer new ideas and new perspectives.

Learning to be more comfortable, open, and responsive to diversity allows us to grow and improve. We invite you to celebrate the diversity of the early childhood professionals you support as well as the young children and families in the program. In that way, each one of us adds a tone to the music of life. The more we are able to value, listen, support, and harmonize every single one of these voices, the more able we are to produce a magnificent symphony.

Revisit the questions on page 3. How have your responses changed? How have they stayed the same?

Competencies

- Understand culture at a deep level (versus touristic approaches).

Practices

- Be interested and curious about cultures.

- Be proactive in learning about your own and your client's culture.

- Be respectful of different cultures.

- Acknowledge that all cultures bring social capital.

- Respond to your client's culture.

- Provide coaching that will support long-lasting, sustainable change.

- Deepen your relationships with your clients.

- Develop stronger rapport.

- Focus on your client's strengths.

- Be present to your client.

- Be equitable with your clients; everyone has different needs.

- Take an active role in identifying and acting against discrimination.

- Celebrate the rich cultural diversity of your clients.

Hear Your Client's Voice

- How can you apply what you have learned in this chapter to be more attuned to your client's voice?

- What are some specific actions you can take the next time you are with your client to hear their voice more clearly?

Hear Your Voice

- Reflect on your current coaching model. Is it transactional, or is it aimed at sustaining long-term change?

- How do the ideas in this chapter affect the way you perceive your current coaching practices?

References and Resources

Hooks, Bell. 1994. *Teaching to Transgress: Education as the Practice of Freedom*. New York: Routledge.

Kuhn, Thomas S. 1970. *The Structure of Scientific Revolutions*. Chicago: University of Chicago Press.

CHAPTER 2

The Coach's Voice

Shifts in how we perceive the world occur because what we
experience changes the questions we ask.

—David Rock and Linda J. Page, *Coaching with the Brain in Mind*

Voices from the Field: Jill

I rang the doorbell and waited a few minutes for Carolyn to open the door. It was
naptime, and I could hear "Twinkle, Twinkle, Little Star" playing on the tablet
on the shelf over the library area. Five weeks into our coaching conversations,
Carolyn and I were still getting to know each other. Although we come from
different backgrounds and experiences, I felt that we had found some common
ground from which to build our relationship. From this foundation, we could
work together to help her achieve the goals she set for herself. As I waited for her
to open the door, our last conversation was running through my head. I felt a
connection as we began to share why we love what we do and what inspires us to
get up in the morning. While listening to her story, the image of her growing up
in an inner-city neighborhood felt familiar yet foreign. I too grew up in an inner
city but in a Latin American country, not the United States. We shared how we
played with our siblings and friends in the street while the adults sat on the door-
steps talking. Life seemed to be safer then and, in many respects, more centered
on family life. She shared her concern over her son's safety and the safety of other
African American boys in her program. She wanted to make sure they were
safe and learned not to talk back to authority. She believed that would help keep
them from getting into trouble. I reflected on how I never had to think about
my son's safety in that way and how much more I needed to learn from her and

understand her experience before any suggestions I made could connect to her reality. It was going to take much more reflection on my part to make visible the filters that may influence my interaction and ultimately connection with Carolyn.

Reflective Questions

- What experiences or people in your life contributed to your understanding of who you are as a person, and how did they influence your values and beliefs?

- How have your own experiences influenced how you interact with others?

- What practices do you follow to put aside your beliefs and values to be empathetic and better understand others?

- What are your biases, hot spots, or things that trigger your reactions?

- Has your sense of self changed over the years? What has stayed constant?

- Have you ever been in a situation where your first impressions of someone were not the correct ones? How did that influence your interaction with that person?

- Who has influenced you, and what did you learn from that person?

Culturally responsive coaching begins with understanding yourself, including your values and practices. We all have a story to tell and a different perspective about what is important as an early childhood professional. For example, the well-being of children is our unifying platform, yet our beliefs about how children learn vary based on our values, knowledge, and experiences. When we understand and make our story visible as coaches, we can better support others to do the same. It also helps us reflect on how much the qualities of who we are influence our perception of our clients and our interactions with them.

This chapter helps us explore who we are as coaches and get to know ourselves first so we can understand others. It is a guide to fostering reflections on our story, including our cultural background, values, and beliefs, and how we put these into practice. By exploring what drives us and why we chose the field of early childhood education and the path of being a coach, we can increase our self-knowledge and deepen our professional commitment and success as influencers of behavior and professional development.

An essential piece of who we are comes from our culture, which influences our beliefs, values, and behaviors. This chapter expands on the meaning of *culture* presented in the first chapter and provides information on what it means to be a culturally responsive coach and how it leads to sustainable change. This process of self-reflection and understanding the behaviors that are influenced by our cultural values, beliefs, and practices mirrors the journey that our clients will go through. This awareness enables us as coaches to be responsive and support our clients' sense of self, mirroring the competencies we want to instill in them.

The intent of taking you through this journey is threefold:

1. The more we understand ourselves, the better we understand our behavior and how we respond to others. This self-reflection, in turn, guides us in gaining control over our reactions and increasing our understanding of others.

2. Self-reflection to more deeply understand our cultural values, beliefs, and temperament tendencies fosters empathy and compassion in ourselves and others.

3. The process of self-reflection and understanding mirrors the behavior we aim to instill in our clients. We need to live the process ourselves before expecting others to do the same.

Throughout this chapter, we present self-reflective questions designed to elicit an internal dialogue about who you are, what drives you, and how your experiences influence your coaching stance. This reflective journey and internal dialogue will, in turn, foster culturally responsive interactions with your clients. These exercises have accompanied us throughout our professional development and draw on emerging research from other fields focused on human development and leadership. For example, brain research increasingly emphasizes that relationships affect learning and development in children and adults. Our understanding of human development also affirms that a culturally responsive coaching process begins when we are aware of our own beliefs and values. We couple this wisdom with our experience working as coaches and leaders who inspire others. We hope we are fueling the torch in you to continue this synergy.

Reflective Practice Begets Reflective Actions

Throughout your career, you may have learned the importance of using reflective questions as a tool to engage in a meaningful conversation, especially when working with other early childhood professionals, but you may not have directed those questions internally. Even if you have practiced self-reflection, your organization's cultural context may not have supported this questioning or given you time to do it. We infuse reflective questions throughout the book to reinforce the importance of this practice in fostering a better understanding of who we are and how we can use that information to engage with others. As we pursue these thoughtful exchanges, we continue wondering how best to connect as we build relationships and undergo intentional transformation with the families, child care educators, teachers, directors, and specialists with whom we work. When we engage in a reflective practice, we strengthen our understanding of why we respond the way we do. We can then be open to listening to what drives the response of others. This practice of self-reflection and analysis also inspires us to share our stories with other coaches or people we have supervised.

Likewise, the practice of ongoing self-reflection and affirmation of who we are is essential to influence change in others. When we model for our clients the same behaviors and attitudes that lead to optimal development in children, they will feel the positive effects and know what these interactions look like in practice. These behaviors of compassion, overall well-being, and reflective practice have to start with us. Getting to know ourselves is a critical part of the process.

As we fine-tune our reflective questions, we can understand what filters we bring as we engage with our clients. The filters that determine how we perceive other people, events, and objects stem from our values, beliefs, and practices as well as our experiences and knowledge gained over time. Filters can cause different people to respond in distinct ways to a shared experience. A workshop facilitator whose filter focuses on compliance might interpret a participant yawning as a sign of disrespect and then remind everyone that they must pay attention. Another facilitator of that same workshop could interpret the yawn through an empathetic lens by acknowledging we all have moments of tiredness and see that it's time to take a stretching break.

What filters do you bring to the table as a coach that influence your interactions with your clients? How do these affect how you ultimately engage in the role of influencer of others? For the remainder of the chapter, we present strategies that answer these questions, practices that have helped us, the authors, in our self-discovery process. They include many interconnected components that we often use to focus on working with others but less frequently on ourselves. Some of these interwoven strategies are internal in nature, while others influence or are influenced by our relationships with others. Listening to ourselves, identifying our motivating drives, and understanding our temperament tendencies requires a process of introspection. Here we offer practices that take this inner awareness and channel it so we can hear the voices of others. Whatever strategy we use, the aim is to support us to know ourselves and increase our understanding and empathy of who we are so we can serve others better.

Free Up Your Mind to Listen to Your Inner Voice

Everyone has different ways of connecting to their inner voice. When we listen to it, we become aware of how our body reacts in different circumstances, fine-tune our sense of who we are, and then reflect on how all of this influences our interaction with others. To build an awareness of how our bodies respond requires us to drown out the noise and distractions that put us on automatic pilot. When we move through space without realizing how we got from point A to point B, we lose control of our movements. To hear our inner voice, we must disconnect from the hustle and bustle so our minds can be decluttered and reenergized to think clearly. These moments become even harder when there are competing demands on our time from children, family members, work, and life in general. Although at times it is hard to find moments that are devoid of distractions, these precious times are essential to help us collect our thoughts, strengthen our senses, and increase awareness of our responses. Just noticing what we are doing, how we are doing it, and how we feel while we move tunes us into ourselves and frees our minds up from what is not immediately in front of us.

Taking a walk around the block to gaze up at the trees or at the architectural details of buildings enhances our ability to see. Listening to the birds or music while driving boosts our auditory senses and helps us listen to others. Even focusing on the mundane movements during daily routines such as what the water feels like as we are taking a shower or the bristles in our mouth as we brush our teeth builds an awareness of our movements and is a way to place the mind on the here and now. Journaling, playing an instrument, or drawing also helps to declutter our minds and become the conduit to the process of awareness.

Strengthening our senses gives us tools to decipher how our bodies respond at other moments, especially when we are stressed. Do our shoulders scrunch up because of what is being said, or are our shoulders straight to show receptiveness? Are we unknowingly frowning because we don't understand or are bothered by what we are hearing? Or are we smiling and sending a message of acceptance? Are our hands relaxed next to our bodies, or are they clenched and folded over to convey that our armor is up? It is amazing how much more in control we are with our responses when we tune in to the present and increase our awareness of these simple movements.

Understand Your Temperament Tendencies and How They Influence Your Interactions

Our biological makeup, along with the experiences and interactions with our environment, contributes to who we are as individuals, including our temperament tendencies. The definition of *temperament* that resonates with us is the natural way that we respond to people, experiences, and interactions with the physical world. Our unique combination of temperament tendencies and experiences shades our perception of our interactions. When we understand how our temperament tendencies influence us, our responses can become more intentional.

These responses develop at an early age and influence our lives way into adulthood. Several temperament tendencies are influenced by our environment and cultural beliefs and practices, including our level of activity, the degree to which we stay on tasks or get easily distracted, how exuberant we are, and even how adaptable we are to change. These temperament tendencies are also perceived differently in various cultural contexts, either at the family, community, or organization level. In some families or cultures, a high level of activity is valued, as it is associated with productivity. Similarly, in other cultures, showing exuberance is accepted as the norm, and demonstration of feelings is often encouraged.

The degree to which your temperament tendencies are aligned with cultural expectations influences your sense of who you are. We each experience life differently, even if we are from the same family, macroculture, or country. For example, my (Jill's) temperament tendency is more withdrawn, and during family gatherings when I was a child I experienced a lot of commotion. People talked at each other in loud voices, while I preferred to listen to music in a quiet room. In contrast, my siblings enjoyed the noisy get-togethers and engaged in conversations with cousins, aunts, and uncles. It was the same experience, yet the interpretation of others and sense of self was very different. When you were little, how did you interpret family gatherings or other events that included other people? Have you ever asked someone who was also at that gathering what their experience was like? You might find that their feelings or memories are completely different.

A variety of resources is readily available to determine your temperament tendencies, some of which we have included at the end of this chapter. As you identify your temperament tendencies, reflect on how this information is another piece of the puzzle of understanding yourself and accepting who you are.

Reflection

What are your temperament tendencies? Have they stayed stable over time? Did your family, friends, or teachers affirm your temperament tendencies when you were a child? What temperament tendencies do you tend to value? Are they different from your clients'?

Define What Drives You

When we identify our life's calling, what drives or motivates us, we can channel that energy to foster well-being and lasting change. It becomes the fuel that keeps us on track. As we focus on what guides our behavior and perceptions, we can become more intentional in filtering out the noise and instead listening to that inner guide that brings us joy and leads to positive outcomes.

We may not always ask ourselves, "What brought me to where I am today? What keeps me motivated?" But the "why" of what we do is essential to keep us motivated—it is something to fall back on during challenging times. In the business world, there is an increased emphasis on supporting executives to identify their personal and corporate "whys" to drive success, ultimately to improve their bottom line. But in early childhood education, a profession focused on human development, it feels as if we are constantly on the go and too busy to reflect on what motivates us, or we have come to believe our personal drive isn't important.

Yet, as with other professions, identifying our "why" helps put the daily routine into perspective and gives us energy to move forward. When we lead with our "why" of what we do, we understand and control our behaviors and are more fulfilled. Many of us came into the profession because we had a true love for children or felt that we could make a difference in the lives of others. However, to truly understand that gut-level energy, we frequently need to affirm that the motivation still stands.

To answer our deeper "why," we need to spend time reflecting on moments that have inspired us, to identify what we value and to discover what we need at a personal and professional level. Similarly, envisioning what we want to be doing in five or ten years gives us a long-term perspective so that we can question whether what we are currently doing will be a conduit to getting there. When we go through this process, we can then empathize with and support our clients to identify their "whys" and pinpoint what they are doing to fuel their drive.

One way that we have found our "why" is by talking with a trusted friend, colleague, or even a career coach to help us identify moments that we felt energized us and contrasted these with times that drained us. We have also explored what it means to get out of your comfort zone, considering whether we are staying in the same place because of fear of the unknown or because we are fulfilled. Identifying your comfort zone and then being brave and moving beyond it to gain new insights and rekindle your drive is essential to not becoming stagnant. We have included resources at the end of this chapter to support your journey in identifying your "why" and understanding your comfort zone.

A LIFE-TURNING EVENT:
Reflections from Jill

We were meeting in Mexico at a big conference center for the annual regional meeting, where we reflected on the past year to begin the new fiscal year's planning process. This trip, however, was different. It had been a tough year. There had been a lot of turnover in the organization, and our team felt the stress caused by the uncertainty surrounding people's jobs. As a team, we felt pulled in many directions, and everyone was overwhelmed with the paperwork. I felt drained and unmotivated to engage in conversations with colleagues. One day, to get away from the tense conference atmosphere, a group of us took a walk during our lunch break. Being outdoors and watching the city's hustle and bustle did wonders for our spirits. We started sharing our experiences of traveling to other countries and reminiscing about our favorite food and restaurants. Just as we were turning the corner at a busy intersection, I saw what appeared to be a family sitting on a bench. A man was holding an infant child, and sitting next to him was a three-year-old boy and his mother. For some reason, that image triggered an energy that I had not felt in a long time. It was as if they were saying, "This image represents why you are working in early childhood." By the end of the walk, I had the beginning of a plan to leave the organization to start my own company so I could directly witness the impact I was having on children and their families.

Reflection

What gets you up in the morning? What are your underlying drives? Are they different from those of your colleagues or workplace? Where and from whom do you get your energy? Where do you see your drive taking you in the future?

Understand Your Values

Our experiences and the cultural messages we receive during our early years influence our values and how we put them into action. Even if we use the same word to describe a commonly shared value, such as *trust*, we may manifest it differently based on our experiences. If you ask people from different cultures to name their top five values, many will include respect. However, when they describe how to show respect, they will give a variety of answers. Some may show respect by greeting everyone one by one as they enter a room. Yet for you it may be enough to wave hi and then walk inside. Respectful body language varies too. For example, in some cultures you hand an object to another person by using both hands and bowing, whereas in others you use only the right hand. Another cultural difference relates to the concept of time. In some cultures the phrase "If you are on time, then you are late" applies. In contrast, in another cultural setting, arriving to a dinner invitation one hour late is the norm.

As we get to know ourselves, we need to name our values and identify what they look like. A simple exercise is to take a piece of paper and draw a line down the middle to form two columns. In the left column, make a list of your values, such as respect, honesty, friendship, belonging, diversity, and so on. (Find resources with examples of other values in the references and resources section at the end of this chapter.) In the right column, make a list of what you would say or do that demonstrates that value. Then fold the paper in half so that you see only the list of values. Have someone else repeat this exercise according to their values and practices. First share and compare the left-hand column to see if there are any similarities. Then open up the paper to compare how these values are demonstrated. It might surprise you to see that even when your values are similar, the behaviors may be very different.

For me (Jill) growing up in Bolivia, respect to elders and unfamiliar people was done by looking down. In contrast, that same value of respect when I came to the United States was manifested by looking people in the eye. Although these conflicting messages were challenging for a child trying to navigate two cultures, it helped me appreciate the importance of listening to understand and looking at situations from different perspectives. When coaching others, I am more conscious now that although we might *say* we have the same value, we may be misinterpreting the manifested behavior.

Reflection

Think back to a time when you felt a conflict with someone. Could it have been because you each had a different way of showing the same value?

Consider early messages you received about learning

We are all born eager to learn, build relationships, and interact with our surroundings. We also came into this world with a genetic makeup that influenced how we took in the information and processed it. The combination of our biological makeup and our environment influenced how and what we learned. As children we learned by exploring, asking questions, falling down and getting up again, and playing with our friends and family members. However, often this inner drive to learn has been stifled by a school system that wanted to teach us the right answer, protect us from making mistakes, and pressure us to conform. As a result, as adults we lost that sense of excitement that comes from learning and figuring out how things work, and the simple pleasure of play.

Interactions with significant people in our lives, whether that was our parents, siblings, teachers, or religious leaders, shaped our understanding of ourselves and our capacity to learn. When adults listened to us, asked for our opinion, and showed how they enjoyed us being together, the message received was "I can do it, what I have to say is important, and I am wanted." When adults told us, "Do as you are told because I said so" or were so busy that they had little time for us, then the message we received may have been "I'm not in control, my opinions don't matter, and other things are more important than I am." The child-rearing practices we experience when we are young often become part of our own child-rearing practices and genetic makeup and get passed down from one generation to another. The back-and-forth interactions between an infant and significant adult can change the way DNA is expressed, which then gets passed on to the next generation. The identification of the multigenerational effects of our behavior is part of the exciting new field of epigenetics. If you are interested in exploring this topic, and especially how it influences our field, the Center on the Developing Child is a good place to start. (See the resource at the end of this chapter for relevant research on this topic.)

These early experiences influence how we perceive learning in adults. Do we promote self-discovery and learning from our clients' experiences and focus on how we can support their learning through our interactions? Or do we focus on what we think we need to teach the educator and correct what they are not doing right? Do we see ourselves as the knower and the client as the blank slate we need to fill? At times we may portray a sense that we know it all and are there to teach because we are the coaches. Yet we know that the best way to learn is through discovery and fostering continuous reflection.

For example, imagine you are working with an educator who continuously asks a child, "What color is the truck?" You might feel yourself tensing because you want them to ask open-ended questions that foster extended conversations rather than closed-ended questions that elicit one or two responses and focus on testing whether someone is right or wrong. Your initial reaction might be to jump in and say, "Those are closed-ended questions. You need to ask a question that supports higher-order thinking so you can get a higher score on your evaluation." When the educator looks at you and agrees but continues to ask the same type of questions, you might feel the educator is stubborn or defiant, or just doesn't get it. In contrast, when you draw from your own innate curiosity to learn and become open to different interpretations, you ask reflective questions to figure out the "why" behind her actions. Questions such as "I wonder what she knows about how children learn" or "I wonder how I can respond in a way to model open-ended questions" can yield powerful answers.

The way we perceive the role of mistakes in the learning process influences how we respond when we fail at something. For example, children who are learning to walk fall many times yet keep trying no matter how many times they fail. It's an innate behavior to keep on trying. Learning to ride a bike or learning to write also engages the iterative process of trying and failing. If we were chastised for not keeping our balance on the bike or not getting a high grade on a writing assignment, the message we received about failing was discouraging. These negative messages can also be self-fulfilling. We fail because we can't, and we can't because we are afraid to fail. On the other hand, if someone showed empathy and encouraged us to get back up on the bike or looked at the writing assignment with us, we would be more likely to keep trying.

How we support learning for our clients is also influenced by how we perceive mistakes or failing. Do we affirm our clients' attempts to try new ways of working with children, if they do not succeed at first, because we understand the importance of trial and error? When we see mistakes or failures as an opportunity to learn, we send messages of encouragement and affirmation to our clients. If we received the messages growing up that falling or not getting it right the first time is a sign of weakness, it could influence our perception of our clients' trials and errors as well as our own failures. We need to constantly remind ourselves that we all make mistakes, and in one way or another we learn from them.

Likewise, when we practice self-compassion and celebrate our mistakes as an essential human trait, we become more empathetic with ourselves and others. Feelings of frustration are part of the growth process—and are okay. When you understand how you respond to making mistakes within a learning context, you can control your responses by reflecting on what you can learn from this experience. This also models for your clients that mistakes are an opportunity to increase your knowledge and competencies to solve similar problems and hopefully not be so hard on yourself.

We model this process by thinking back to when we made a mistake or something went wrong and considering how we responded to and used that experience. For example, if you got lost in a new neighborhood, do you resist driving there again, or do you reflect on how that experience will help you learn how to get there the next time? Reflections help us cement our mindset to perceive these mishaps as learning opportunities. They give us ideas for how we might react the next time we make a mistake or face conflict. How might we respond when there is a disconnect with our client? Do we try to look at the situation from different perspectives and learn from the disconnect, or do we just plunge ahead, expecting the other person to change? The choice is ours.

Reflection

What messages about learning did you receive growing up? Was your inner drive to learn valued and affirmed, or was it stifled so you would conform? What messages did you receive from the significant adults in your life about your learning capacity? Did they value your ideas and encourage you to share your thoughts and experiences? What messages did you receive early in life about making mistakes? Should making a mistake or engaging in a conflict be avoided at all costs? Or did you come to understand that you made mistakes because you were not trying hard enough or were not good enough? Or did you learn that mistakes are part of a necessary iterative process of trying, failing, and problem solving in order to finally succeed, like baking or learning to drive? How much do you value mistakes or challenging situations as an opportunity to learn?

Show vulnerability and self-compassion

Demonstrating our vulnerability and practicing self-compassion are two essential competencies in a culturally responsive coaching process. Both help us build inner strength and increase feelings of acceptance, affirmation, and empathy. No matter who we are, at some point in our lives we have experienced vulnerability, whether personal, economic, or social. Perhaps when you started a new job, you felt uncertain about what was expected of you and worried whether you could be successful. Starting a new relationship, you may have wondered whether you were compatible with your partner and whether it would work out. If you or a loved one became seriously ill, you wondered whether you or they would ever recover. You may also have felt vulnerable when you have worked with clients who look, act, or feel differently than you, fearful that you would not understand each other or that there would be personality clashes.

With vulnerability, we open ourselves to showing that we can be hurt or negatively affected by situations or other people. Being vulnerable can be associated with weakness. By admitting that we are vulnerable, we might feel like we are saying we are not strong enough to deal with these challenges. The end result is that we drown out these feelings or blame others as an escape, so we are not at fault for the situation or failure. How we respond to these vulnerabilities affects our overall well-being and sense of self-worth. When you accept that we are all vulnerable, this acceptance makes visible what scares or negatively affects you. In contrast, by hiding our vulnerabilities we pretend that they don't exist, which is not the same as being strong. We may think that we are strong, but we are actually stronger when we face our vulnerabilities and find ways to address them. The strength comes from admitting our vulnerabilities and knowing that they don't control us. When we can see them, then we can do something to change the situation, and having this control lowers our angst and stress level. Acknowledging our vulnerabilities can also be a sign of strength because we have the self-confidence to put them out in the open where others may see them. When we embrace our vulnerability, accept it as a human trait, and learn from it, we become stronger. However, if we do not accept our vulnerabilities or blame others for our troubles, we become weak and ineffective in dealing with them.

Our upbringing and cultural practices that emphasize either cooperation or competitiveness influence how we respond to our vulnerabilities. If we are taught that failure is a weakness or that we can't show others our weaknesses because they will take advantage of them, we lose the power to make change happen. On the other hand, when we can share our vulnerabilities with our clients and talk about how we continue to overcome them, we build trust and openness for them to share their own vulnerabilities and accept support.

Vulnerability and self-compassion both influence how we respond to and cope with different situations. Although vulnerability and self-compassion might seem to be at the opposite ends of the continuum of feelings, one leading to fear and the other to comfort, they are intertwined by how they influence each other. Self-compassion is an antidote for vulnerability. When we practice self-compassion, it helps us understand that being vulnerable is part of being alive. When we think back to moments in our lives when we were scared, insecure, or lost, consider how differently those moments could have felt if we'd had an inner voice that said, "These feelings are normal," "You are going through a rough time right now," "Be kind to yourself; you will figure it out." We would have received the understanding and support to move forward. Yet when we are most vulnerable, we tend not to practice self-compassion.

How we practice self-compassion is also influenced by our upbringing and early experiences. If you were given the message that you are worthy of care, then self-compassion may come easily. If you received a message that the well-being of others came first and taking care of your needs was being selfish, being kind to yourself may take more effort. How we feel about ourselves and our actions tends to influence how we respond to others. As you continue your self-reflection journey, notice how you react when you feel vulnerable. Focus on your breath by slowly inhaling and exhaling while sitting still and listening to the sounds around you for a few minutes. This mindfulness exercise gets oxygen into your body and helps you become aware of how you feel.

When we are kind to ourselves, practice mindfulness, and acknowledge that being stressed out and making mistakes are human traits, we can reduce the amount of cortisol in our bodies, which inhibits neural transmission and higher-order thinking (Fuochi, Veneziani, and Voci 2018). Organizations and researchers from different disciplines echo these conclusions, including the Center on the Developing Child, Self-Compassion Organization (Neff n.d.), and researcher Brené Brown, who studies vulnerability and courage. A list of relevant articles is included at the end of the chapter for you to deepen your knowledge of how vulnerabilities, stress, self-compassion, and learning are interrelated.

Reflection

What early messages have influenced your perception of vulnerability and self-compassion? Do you embrace your vulnerabilities? Do you use them to overcome challenges? How do you transmit these messages to your clients? Are you able to anticipate these feelings and understand how they can affect your work with clients? What are the values in your culture that support or inhibit your practice of self-compassion?

Show empathy instead of sympathy

Although *empathy* and *sympathy* sound similar and are often confused, each leads to a different outcome in ourselves and others. Empathy involves understanding and putting ourselves in someone else's shoes, while sympathy involves feeling sorry for someone and to some extent taking pity on them. The way we demonstrate each of these through our words and our actions is very different. When we empathize, we say, "I hear you; I understand you." We can empathize when someone is expressing sorrow, anger, and frustration as well as happiness, joy, gratitude, or love, feelings that are felt across cultures. When we empathize, we validate the other person and connect to that person on an equal footing. We too have felt that way, even if the experiences that caused those feelings were not the same. We all have felt confused, frustrated, sad, happy, angry, and joyful at some point in our lives, and we can draw from those experiences to understand what the other person is feeling. It's in the understanding from others that we find the inner strength and validation to make change happen.

On the other hand, the way we show sympathy is through words such as "I'm sorry," "You poor thing," and "What happened to you is terrible." The feelings that prompt sympathy are associated with loss, sorrow, and mishap. It's not to say that feelings of sympathy are wrong; it's that they don't have the same empowering effect as when we empathize.

Empathy involves sharing our feelings and vulnerabilities and sends the message that the other person is not alone. It puts aside our differences and places us in the other person's shoes without judgment or biases. It involves seeing the whole person as a capable human being, looking beyond the situation that they are in.

So how do we practice empathy? What do we need to know about ourselves so that our interactions are empathetic and lead to connection? First, be aware of your responses when a client shares an emotional experience. For example, do you feel your body moving away or your mind distancing itself, perhaps wanting to take the discomfort away quickly? Or do you feel yourself lean into the conversation, listening to understand what your client is saying without judgment? Next, be conscious about the words you use to respond. An empathetic response will convey a message of connection, such as "I hear you. It's not easy at this time for you; you sound overwhelmed." And last, be present for the other person by putting aside any distractions or agendas to focus on the person in front of you.

Psychiatrist Helen Riess, who researches empathy, has spelled out key behaviors that we can learn to be more empathetic. She has seen the life-changing impact in her patients, and we have seen a huge difference in our work with clients. The actions of really seeing the other person and becoming aware of what our expressions, movements, and tone of voice are conveying are essential to showing empathy. In a 2013 TedTalk, Riess ended her presentation on the power of empathy with these words: "We all need to see each other to bring out the full potential in others—their specialness reflected back in the eyes of others in order to see it themselves" (Riess 2013).

Reach out to others

Having a community of peers brings clarity and can reenergize us through the bumps in the road. Sharing our thoughts, bouncing around ideas, and having our voices played back to us helps us feel heard so that we in turn can hear others. In working with clients, we encounter moments when there is a disconnect between what we say and the actions we, or others, take in response. A colleague can help you talk about issues and offer another perspective, leading to alternative ways to engage with your client. A colleague can restate what they think was said or done that could have been misinterpreted, giving you a glimpse of how your words or actions are perceived by others. For example, if you keep looking at your watch during a coaching session, maybe you are trying to be mindful of the client's time. But your actions may be perceived as your wanting the meeting to be over. Having someone we trust to talk through different perspectives with us helps us see how others hear us, and in turn this opens us to listening to others.

Reflection

Do you have colleagues whom you can reach out to for support and feedback? How has having (or not having) someone to bounce ideas off of influenced your coaching? Have you supported a colleague in this way? How did that influence their interactions with their clients?

Understand the power your words and daily interactions have on your client

As coaches, supervisors, and directors, we have a crucial role in early childhood educators' lives. The way we interact, what we say, and the nonverbal communication we use influences others. Even the most minor comments or gestures can ignite the spark that makes a lasting or significant difference—or can blow that spark out. When we are aware of the gestures and the words we use, we can be more intentional in choosing which ones we apply in different circumstances. For example, nuances in how we work with a client who has asked us to look at their environment will lead to different outcomes. If we start by looking at a checklist and spelling out everything that needs to change in an environment, we transmit the message that we value the checklist and that we know the answers and they don't. However, if we begin with reflective questions, learning the children's ages, how they use the space, which areas of the room work well, and which areas don't, through our mannerisms we recognize that they have knowledge and we are a facilitator in making it visible. The subtle difference in asking questions that provoke reflection, versus seeking a right or wrong answer, influences our clients immensely. When we engage as learners, we are open to listening and learning more about the situation, and we send the message that we are partners. When we present ourselves as the knower, we ultimately create dependency, self-doubt, and short-term change. Sustainable change comes, however, when what we say and do transmits the message that the client is the keeper of the knowledge.

From the first time we receive their contact information, every moment that we interact with our clients influences them. Our first contact is critical, and we must be intentional in how it takes place. For example, you might send out a form letter letting new clients know that you will be their coach. This strategy could be efficient, and it would ensure that everyone gets the same message, but it is one-directional. However, if you take the time to call each of your clients to introduce yourself, it may take longer, but it starts building a relationship from the get-go. The more we realize how our words and actions influence others, the more intentional we will be about walking the walk and aligning what we do with our values.

Be a servant leader

Leadership is the process of motivating others to achieve a common goal. It has nothing to do with your position, level of seniority, or ability to tell people what to do. A true leader makes things happen by energizing, supporting, and engaging others. As coaches and early childhood educators, we become leaders when we motivate others toward the goal of fostering optimal learning and development. Our mission as leaders is to serve others and look out for their well-being. We influence the lives of others not by commanding but by building trusting relationships through our interactions and fostering meaningful experiences. In a culturally responsive coaching relationship, leadership that leads to sustainable change follows the model of a servant leader. Servant leadership involves listening, reflecting, and guiding the learning process through empathy and humility. We listen, focused on understanding a client's perspective by showing humility and being grounded in their reality. We promote a client's well-being, problem-solving skills, and autonomy because we know and respect them as a competent professional. We may have knowledge and experience that our clients don't have, yet they know themselves and their environment much better than we do. They are also the ones ultimately responsible for driving the changes they make; if they aren't in the driver's seat, then changes will be short-lived.

Pause your assumptions so you can really hear the other person

An essential element of a culturally responsive coaching framework is understanding the perspective of your client so that you can meet them where they are. Yet it is difficult to do that when our minds are busy coming to conclusions about what the other person is trying to say or do. We often see people based on what has been ingrained in our heads, beginning from an early age when we heard messages and stereotypes from the adults around us categorizing or judging others based on their appearance, skin color, or economic level. We first must understand our hidden biases so that we can take stock of how our responses are influenced by our perceptions of others.

When your biases become visible, you can control them and make changes that open communication and understanding as you work with your clients. Ask others you trust who know you well to mirror back your behaviors so you become aware of these unconscious biases. Having someone repeat what you said and the way they heard it helps you hear yourself from the other person's perspective. You become aware of automatic mannerisms. The next step is to acknowledge that you are not alone in this process. Your peers, mentors, and community at large are resources to increase your knowledge and understanding of these uncomfortable and stirring feelings that come from the realization that unconscious biases have a detrimental effect on our behavior and that of others.

As a woman who grew up in two macrocultures, Latin America and the United States, I (Jill) often reflect on how my racial and cultural backgrounds are molded into one, and it's difficult for me to see where one ends and the other begins. I have become aware of the way I interact in different circumstances and with different people only after receiving feedback from others. I'm fluent in

English and Spanish, and it is natural for me to switch back and forth between the two. However, when I began to reflect on how I feel when I speak English versus Spanish, I realized that there was a difference in my interactions. I feel a special connection from the heart with people when I speak Spanish—it seems to tap into a part of my brain that elicits trust, comfort, and acceptance. On the other hand, when I am speaking in English, especially with people I don't know, I've been told that I sound academic, dry, and void of passion, and it takes me a while to make a connection. But this is far from the truth of who I think I am! This awareness was put into practice as I began to write this book, which is intended to be conversational in nature. To silence my academic, more rigid side while writing, I put on Spanish music to keep that side of my brain engaged.

Reflection

As you engage with clients who are of the same racial, ethnic, linguistic, or cultural background as you, think about how your nonverbal communication contributes to that interaction. Is it the same or different from when you engage with people who look, talk, think, or act differently from you? Are you aware of how your mannerisms are perceived and affect others?

Self-reflect on your biases, values, and perceptions

As we shared in chapter 1, understanding our own biases, values, and perceptions is essential in our work as coaches. This understanding is especially critical in the early childhood field, as we are able to influence well-being and foster respect across the life span. Humans come in all shapes, sizes, and races, with knowledge about who they are and whom they want to be with. Some people have characteristics that are completely different from our own, including some that do not align with our cultural, religious, economic, or political values. Yet we all are humans who have an important role to play in the well-being of current and future generations. It is our diversity that makes us resilient and has contributed to the expansion of the human species.

That diversity, however, can also bring fear, anger, hate, and violence as we encounter others who are different from us. The ongoing Black Lives Matter movement and then the deaths of Breonna Taylor and George Floyd in 2020 reinforced the truth that racism is ever present. It also brought to the forefront the need to address the effects that white privilege (which influences the opportunities you have based on whether your skin is light or dark) has on everyone's lives. The long-term cost of not investing in equity is too great. As humans, and as a society, we are stronger when our diversity is valued and is woven into the foundation of what we do. When everyone has the same chances of reaching their potential, everyone can contribute to a thriving society. Whether we are conscious of it or not, the way we look, our beliefs, and who we love affects the way we are treated and treat others.

The increased visibility of the racially motivated violence fueled by white supremacy put into question the value that we, as a society, place on equity, justice, and compassion. As early childhood professionals, we have an ethical and moral responsibility to take a stand to ensure that *everyone* is treated with human dignity, that we continuously strive to uncover and address our unconscious biases, and that we affirm that we all have the same rights and privileges. How we perceive race and equity influences our response to the loss of human life. How we interact with others on a daily basis, especially when they look different, speak another language, have different abilities, or don't share the same sexual orientation or gender identity or expression as us, is a mirror of who we want to be.

Unpacking our perceptions and how we feel about people who are different from us is essential to really hear all voices, not only in early childhood settings but across our communities. This process of unpacking requires reflecting and making visible who we are, what we believe in, and where we discover disconnects with others. When we understand ourselves, we can then connect with others by understanding and respecting the essence of who they are. The process can be a painful one, which can lead us to deny our feelings or actions because of the guilt or helplessness it can evoke. Or it can be taken on as a journey of discovery, reconciliation, and action at a personal and community level.

We first explore who we are and the origins of what we believe in and what we value. There are numerous ways to discover our biases, either by directly interacting with people or by using tools such as online tests. You may want to begin by asking family members about their experiences growing up and the values and beliefs that were transmitted to them. We can next listen to people who are different from us to hear and understand their stories. How did their experiences influence their beliefs and values? Did they grow up in an environment that promoted stereotypes or biases toward them or others?

To reduce our prejudices and truly hear others' voices, we must put on hold our automatic perceptions of what the other person is like. For example, if you come from a predominantly white community, you may have heard or experienced conflict involving people of color and assumed that a person was acting a certain way because of their race. Likewise, you may be working with clients who come from a country that you associate with laziness or violence. By putting these thoughts and beliefs on hold, you can become more open to listening to the other person without prejudices, with the intent to understand and learn from your confusion. It is amazing how often we find that we are much more alike than we are different.

This self-reflection may include using tools such as the Harvard Education Implicit Association Test (IAT) (see the Project Implicit link at the end of this chapter) to uncover unconscious biases. This tool has had controversial response, so if you are going to take the test, read the disclaimer before starting it.

Put on your mask first

Although we are a caring profession, taking care of our own needs is easier said than done. When you travel by plane, at the beginning of each flight you hear the instruction, "Put your oxygen mask on first before assisting others." The premise behind this safety instruction is that you will be of no help to others if you cannot breathe. Although this seems to be sound advice, putting it into practice is, as the saying goes in Spanish, "Entre el dicho y el hecho hay mucho trecho" (In between saying something and doing it, there is a huge void). As early childhood professionals and as coaches in particular, this seems especially to be the case. Even though as coaches our focus is on the well-being of the educators we work with, we also need to take care of our own needs.

Finding the right mix of physical, nutritional, and mindful well-being is a challenge, yet once we locate that sweet spot, we are so much better off. As a coach of early childhood educators, you may find yourself meeting in the classroom or family child care environment. Your physical movement may be limited to when you are playing with the children as you model a particular interaction. Getting up and down from chairs that are low off the floor may be a struggle at times. Maintaining your body's range of movement and exercising regularly will keep you agile mentally and physically.

As we were writing this book, we were in the middle of the COVID-19 pandemic. In a couple of days, we went from walking, traveling, and eating out without thinking twice to being confined to our homes. This sudden change from activity to isolation was difficult for many, especially for those who get their energy from being around others. It also taught us to appreciate our health and living in the moment. Our resilience was fueled by our virtual connections and knowing that by taking care of ourselves we were contributing to the well-being of others.

Reflection

How did the COVID-19 pandemic affect how you feel about yourself and others? What do you do when you are not feeling well? How do you reenergize?

Revisit the questions on page 18. How have your responses changed? How have they stayed the same?

Competencies

- Engage in self-reflection.

- Practice self-compassion.

- Embrace being a learner.

- Accept being vulnerable.

- Name your values.

- Name your trigger points.

- Practice self-care.

- Accept who you are and celebrate your uniqueness.

Practices

- Practice mindfulness to be in tune with your sense of self in the moment. The more you are aware of your reactions, the more you can control them.

- Be kind to yourself so that you can be open to hearing others' perspectives.

- Show empathy versus sympathy.

- Reflect on your story, including your unconscious biases, cultural background, values, and beliefs and how you put them into practice.

- Identify your temperament tendencies and how these align with your cultural perspectives on what is important.

- Reflect on why you chose the field of early childhood education and the path of being a coach.

- Reflect on the skills, strengths, and abilities you bring to the coaching process and how they influence your perception of others. (See the resources section for two items related to our temperament tendencies and our unconscious bias that we have used to reflect continuously on what we bring to the table. Note how these evolve over time.)

Hear Your Client's Voice

- What questions do you have about applying this chapter to your work with educators from diverse backgrounds and varied early childhood settings? What information and resources are applicable for your client to share with the families, children, and colleagues with whom they work?

Hear Your Voice

- How much of what you read in the chapter is new to you? What questions do you still have about the importance of hearing and understanding your voice?

Hear Other Stakeholders

- How can you use the information presented in this chapter to enhance your interactions with families, colleagues, supervisors, or your own family?

References and Resources

Allred, Keith W., and Christine L. Hancock. 2015. "Leadership: Supporting a New Generation of Early Childhood Professionals." https://fpg.unc.edu/sites/fpg.unc.edu/files/resources /presentations-and-webinars/YC0515_Leadership_and_Partnership_Allred%20(1).pdf.

Brown, Brené. 2020. "List of Values." Dare to Lead website. https://daretolead.brenebrown .com/wp-content/uploads/2020/02/Values.pdf.

Center on the Developing Child, Harvard University. n.d. "Epigenetics and Child Development: How Children's Experiences Affect Their Genes." https://developingchild .harvard.edu/resources/what-is-epigenetics-and-how-does-it-relate-to-child -development.

Fuochi, Giulia, Chiara A. Veneziani, and Alberto Voci. 2018. "Exploring the Social Side of Self-Compassion: Relations with Empathy and Outgroup Attitudes." *European Journal of Social Psychology* 48:769–83. https://self-compassion.org/wp-content/uploads/2019/08 /Fuochi2018.pdf.

International Coaching Federation. n.d. "ICF Core Competencies Rating Levels." https:// coachingfederation.org/app/uploads/2017/12/ICFCompetenciesLevelsTable.pdf.

———. 2021. "Video Series: Updated ICF Core Competencies (2021)." www.youtube.com /playlist?list=PLMBtOVpaN5DjRt-VAJIa0Xe0MLuA-LZNk.

Learning for Justice. n.d. "Test Yourself for Hidden Bias." https://www.learningforjustice.org /professional-development/test-yourself-for-hidden-bias.

Moore, Margaret. n.d. "Guess How a Leader's Humility Promotes Positive Outcomes." www .instituteofcoaching.org/resources/guess-how-leaders-humility-promotes-positive -outcomes.

Neff, Kristin. n.d. "Self-Compassion." https://self-compassion.org/the-research/#areaofstudy.

Newton, Emily, Elita Amini Virmani, J. Ronald Lally, and Peter Mangione for the Program for Infant/Toddler Care. 2019. "Temperament Tendencies." WestEd. https://wested.ent.box .com/s/wy2imm5j97p8o96a6fqsdw44xeqt81mm.

Project Implicit. n.d. "Featured Task: How We Think about Race/Ethnicity." https://implicit .harvard.edu/implicit/featuredtask.html.

Riess, Helen. 2013. "The Power of Empathy." TedxMiddlebury. www.youtube.com /watch?v=baHrcC8B4WM.

———. 2018. *The Empathy Effect: 7 Neuroscience-Based Keys for Transforming the Way We Live, Love, Work and Connect across Differences.* Boulder, CO: Sound True.

Rock, David, and Linda J. Page. 2009. *Coaching with the Brain in Mind.* Hoboken, NJ: Wiley.

The Royal Society for Arts, Manufactures and Commerce. 2013. "Brené Brown on Empathy." www.thersa.org/video/shorts/2013/12/brene-brown-on-empathy.

The School of Life. n.d. "Six Ideas from Eastern Philosophy." www.theschooloflife.com /thebookoflife/six-ideas-from-eastern-philosophy.

Washington State Department of Children, Youth and Families. 2019. "Relationship-Based Professional Development Standards." www.dcyf.wa.gov/sites/default/files/pdf /RBPDStandards.pdf.

CHAPTER 3

The Client's Voice

I celebrate myself, and sing myself,

And what I assume you shall assume,

For every atom belonging to me as good belongs to you.

—Walt Whitman, "Song of Myself," *Leaves of Grass*

Voices from the Field: Erika

I remember the first time I met Martha Argelia. She was a firecracker. Her face was full of energy, excitement, and attentiveness. She was incredibly happy about her new role as a coach for an innovative project that was rolling out across the state, including rural areas that tended to be difficult to reach. Many Spanish-speaking educators would receive coaching through this project, including family child care providers. Supporting this segment of early childhood educators was one of Martha Argelia's biggest passions, due to her own personal history. I was honored to be her coaching mentor during the implementation of this professional development project.

Getting to know Martha Argelia in a deep way was key to supporting her in this innovative endeavor. She was originally from Nicaragua. As a young woman she emigrated with her spouse and children, trying to find a country to live where there would be stability and positive possibilities for her and her family. It was a long journey, but she eventually was able to immigrate to the United States. Here she had to go through the lengthy process of learning how to speak English and learning a new culture and new rules: how to drive, how to communicate with other people, how to register her children for school, what the schools expected of her and her children, and so on. She had a career back at home, but her degree was not immediately recognized in her new country. She struggled but eventually was able to adapt to her new life.

With a keen sense of social justice, her goal was to empower Spanish-speaking educators so that in turn they could provide the best quality education to Spanish-speaking children. Her values were noticeably clear: she was driven by a mission to create a more equitable society. She brought her own story into conversations with the clients she coached and also tried to learn about their stories, believing this would motivate them to improve their practices so that young children would have the best education possible. Because she took the time to know her clients deeply, she was able to form authentic and trustworthy relationships with them.

In a parallel process, I also took the time to get to know Martha Argelia at a deep level. We had many opportunities to speak about her culture, her heritage, and her story. Knowing her deeply was the foundation of the support I could provide her as her coach. For example, different aspects of her culture were reflected in how she coached and took part within the project. Whenever anything happened that she considered unfair or inequitable, she had the strength to bring it up and share it with the group of coaches and the supervising teams as well. She in turn supported her clients to have the courage to share their voices, even when it felt uncomfortable to do so.

A lot of my role as her support was to listen to and acknowledge her feelings when she was angry or anxious. This especially happened whenever she felt little hope of effecting real change. Hours and hours of conversations went on throughout our work together in the coaching relationship. By my accepting, affirming, encouraging, and acknowledging her story and her values, she was successful in supporting the teachers she coached, making a positive change within her organization. I like to think that this in turn also helped empower young children and their families.

Reflective Questions

- How deeply do you know your clients?

- What is the difference between a surface-level relationship versus an authentic, deep-level relationship with coaching clients?

- How can you develop deeper knowledge of your client's background, strengths, and needs?

- How well do you understand your client's culture?

- How do you use your client's culture, history, and professional background to support the coaching process?

One of the goals of coaching is to help your client achieve their fullest potential. This is crucial in early childhood education so that your client in turn can support the full potential of young children. Your client has gone through a long history of experiences related to the field as well as in their own personal lives. As a coach, you are there to serve and support the client and offer whatever they need to grow. Culturally responsive coaching in early childhood requires hearing, understanding, and responding to the client's voice. As a professional in early childhood education, you know the importance of taking the child's perspective to help them grow and develop. In coaching, we likewise need to understand the perspective of the client.

In this chapter, we delve into understanding the significant role of early childhood educators and provide you the opportunity to reflect on understanding who the client is as a person, what drives them, and what factors can influence the change process. You will also be able to reflect on making a connection and building from the client's personal history, culture, education, and professional experiences to weave this understanding into a deeper relationship, thus achieving a more responsive and effective change process. To wholly fulfill the goal of coaching, take the time to understand deeply where the client is and build from there. How could it be otherwise? This chapter offers strategies on how to start getting to know the client and build your support as their coach.

Likewise, take this opportunity to think more deeply about the other stakeholders in the coaching journey, including children and families and the culture of the organization. Reflect on their cultural backgrounds, struggles, dreams, and needs, and consider strategies to better understand their social identities. The celebration of "self" is emphasized throughout the chapter.

Be Present to Your Client

Our time on earth is quite short. Our life span is limited, and each day is precious. Think about how special it is to have the opportunity to use your time to be with your client. This is also your client's time. One of the most valuable treasures we have is time. Try to be fully present to your client and their story. This requires you to be aware of yourself in the moment when you are with your client. Notice your body posture. Do you have any tension in your body, or is it relaxed? Be aware of your feelings in the moment. Are you feeling excited, nervous, uncomfortable, grateful? Observe your thoughts. Are they directed toward understanding what your client is saying? Or are they thinking of something unrelated? Be aware of the surroundings. Is sunlight coming in through the window, is there noise in the hallway, are birds chirping outside the window? Be aware of your breath, and be in the moment, instant by instant. Be aware of your client. Observe your client's body language, listen to each word they say, and consider how they feel. Each client is a human being who has gone through extraordinary experiences that have brought them to this moment. Be aware of the wonderful person in front of you. Accept, embrace, and value your client and their story. This sense of full awareness and acceptance makes each moment of your work as a coach valuable and meaningful. From there we can build meaningful change in the field of early childhood education.

Being Client-Centered

Many of the best practices we use to teach children can be applied in a parallel process with adults, including your clients. When a teacher is centered on a child's perspectives, ideas, interests, motivations, and needs, they are more able to support that child in reaching the next stage of development. The child is at the center of all the curriculum and implementation. The teacher takes into consideration the child's interests and ideas to inform teaching practices.

In a parallel process, we invite you to take a client-centered perspective. Dedicate ample time during your coaching sessions to ask questions about your client's interests and needs as an early childhood professional. Ask them what they love about their work and which aspects of their work they enjoy the most, and why. Find out which are the most challenging aspects of their job. Ask what wakes them up at night. Infuse this knowledge into your coaching process to center it on the client. Doing so will engage your client in the coaching process, which can lead to more progress as you work together toward coaching goals.

The organization you work for may have set up goals for your coaching relationship. But at the same time, find out what your client's actual goals are and consider how they align or intertwine with the organization's goals. This is similar to our work with young children. We know there are certain developmental stages that children go through, and as teachers we try to align a child's interests and perspectives with helping them reach their developmental milestones.

Imagine having a relationship with a client on such a level where hopes, goals, and dreams are shared freely at the heart of the coaching process. So much more can be achieved than if you had only superficial knowledge and a shallow relationship with your client. As a coach, your role is to serve your client, so they need to be at the center of all the work you do.

Reflection

What is your client currently concerned with? What keeps your client up at night? What are your client's dreams for the future? What does your client love? What inspires your client? What does your client love the most about their profession in early childhood?

The Client's Early Childhood Years

Our early years have a deep impact on the rest of our lives. As early childhood educators, we well know that even during the prenatal time, an unborn person's life is already affected by the life events of the mother and other members of the family. Your client's cultural experiences with their families and communities during their earliest years made an imprint, affecting their views regarding themselves, other colleagues, young children, families, and so on. Indeed, experiences and ideas from your client's early childhood years may interfere with their progress toward their goals. Learning more about your client's early childhood may give you knowledge you can use positively to help your client reach goals or overcome barriers.

Consider asking your clients to tell you more about the people they remember who made the most positive impact in their early years. It is amazing to hear the memories that clients share when they hear such a question. You may ask them to tell you what those adults said or did that made such a positive impact. As your client remembers positive moments, big insights and connections can form when they start seeing parallels between these examples and the traits they want to model for young children.

Reflection

When you were a child, who had a positive impact on you? What did that person say or do that was special? How do these experiences affect your current work in the field of early childhood education?

Some clients have few or no positive memories of their early childhood years. Some even say they have no memories of their early years at all. There may be several reasons for this. For example, one's cognitive development may affect the ability to store and/or retrieve memories, or a person's memories have faded over time. However, sometimes traumatic early childhood experiences interfere with people's ability to remember. These adverse early childhood experiences can continue affecting them as adults. However, it is possible to heal through intentional work. It requires strong support systems, awareness, consciousness, and compassion.

If you do work with a client who says they do not remember anything from their early childhood years, they may instead be able to remember adults who had a positive impact on their later years, in high school or when they were beginning their career in early childhood education. The point is to connect these positive experiences to the current work they are doing with young children.

The Client's Heritage and Family History

To get to know your client at a deeper level, you may also wish to learn about
their heritage and family history. These two are tightly connected to your client's
culture. Getting to know their history may help increase your responsiveness to
their culture and create more sustainable long-term change through the coaching
process.

It can be remarkably interesting to converse with a client about where their
family comes from. For example, one of my (Erika's) clients was born in Venezuela, and her family immigrated to Colombia because of conflicts in their home
country, eventually immigrating to the United States. This client was a young
child when she immigrated to the United States, but her family's cultural heritage
made a deep imprint on who she is today. It also affects how she supports other

early childhood educators and children. Her history in Venezuela and Colombia is part of the cultural makeup she brings to her everyday interactions. To know this about my client helped me connect more deeply with her and understand how she in turn relates to young children and to other professionals in the field. Knowing this also helped me see how she can connect with her clients who have similar immigration stories.

Humanity has always faced extreme changes and difficulties, including a long history of discrimination, hate, wars, and other troubles. Traumatic events may have made an imprint in your client's current state of being. As a coach, you cannot ignore that these factors affect how your client reaches their goals. You will see that some clients have built more resiliency because of their family heritage and history, while other clients are still deeply affected physically, emotionally, mentally, and spiritually, based on this history. Having open conversations, sharing about each other's family history, and having empathy for their story can help deepen your relationship and thus support the coaching process.

The Client's Essence

You may also deepen your relationship with the client by finding out more about their interests and preferences. You might inquire about hobbies or other activities they like to do when they have free time. You can also discuss different types of temperament, as described in chapter 2. By doing so, you will learn more about how your client prefers to interact with other adults, including you and their coworkers.

In addition, you may want to consider your client's preferred learning styles. Some clients are more visual, others more auditory, and others more kinesthetic. You may find that some clients learn better through hearing specific examples and others through asking introspective questions. Whatever you discover can help you better approach them during the coaching process.

Dive a little deeper and learn what in the client's essence was most attracted to working in the field of early childhood education. Get to know what they love about children, what they love about working with families, what they love about human development and helping other individuals reach their highest potential. By tapping into this love, we can connect more deeply with our goals for the coaching process and ignite the motivation that is needed to fuel change.

The Client's Culture

Everyone has their own culture. Being culturally responsive begins with an awareness of one's own cultural and social identities. Helping your client become more aware of diverse identities can also support them in better connecting with children's and families' cultures and social identities. Take the time to learn about different identities that may be important to your client, such as nationality, race, gender identity and expression, sexual orientation, ability, religion, beliefs, and values. Have authentic and real conversations with your client about their culture as well as any beliefs they may hold about other identities or cultures. This may help uncover any negative stereotypes that may be affecting the client's work. It is amazing how change can happen by just bringing awareness of negative stereotypes.

In a similar, parallel process, you may also want to talk with your client about the diverse cultural backgrounds of the children and families who are served by the early education program. Talk about what they know about these cultures, including any similarities or differences they recognize, and discuss ways to better connect with people who are different. For example, you may want to point out how you are showing cultural responsiveness toward the client by getting to know their many identities. You show authentic curiosity and interest in your client's story. You acknowledge that you respect and see value in the client's culture. You may point out many similarities you share. Then you may suggest to your client to follow a similar process with others as a way to expand the practices of cultural responsiveness. By doing so, we are setting the stage for cultural responsiveness and equity across all levels within the organization.

The Client's Earlier Professional Experiences

Any experience your client had in the past related to early childhood can be affecting them today. This may also affect the coaching relationship. For example, some clients had positive and warm support from their leadership team, supervisors, and former coaches and mentors. They may start up the coaching conversation with you being open, comfortable, and happy to get going with the learning and development. However, some clients have had less positive experiences in the past. Perhaps they had supervisors who told them exactly what they must do or a coach who did not really help them feel understood or supported. They may think that people who come to coach are really coming to check compliance, and they might be afraid they will lose their job. You can start by asking your client whether they have ever had a coach before. Ask them about their prior coaching experiences. Talk about the experiences you have had with the people who support you, such as a center director or administrator or the school district. When you have an open conversation about this, you are showing your client that you are hearing their voice and valuing their experiences.

All of your client's experiences add up to their culture and will influence your coaching relationship. Invite them to discuss these earlier experiences, and truly listen to them. Being empathetic is key to letting your client know that you understand how they feel and what they have gone through, be it positive or less so.

The Client's Perspectives on Early Childhood Education

It is always interesting to learn about other people's perspectives and beliefs about early childhood education. Diverse cultures have different expectations for how children should learn and develop. Try to find out about your client's early childhood experiences and how they connect with their current beliefs about children. For example, in some cultures caregivers are expected to provide everything to young children, so perhaps a client from such a culture holds this perspective. What happens when we come as a coach and talk about helping children develop more autonomy and independence? Your client might be surprised by the different perspective about children's self-sufficiency and ability to make their own decisions. You will need to have a conversation about your client's earlier experiences and beliefs and how they connect to their practice currently to understand any discrepancies between your perspectives. During these conversations, you may want to share research-based practices, putting forward an invitation to try out various types, observe the results over time, and based on that, reflect on them. It may be that the client finds a strategy you suggested to be effective and adds it into their practice. But perhaps they find it ineffective and question the strategy itself, propose other strategies, or challenge cultural perspectives that may have influenced the research. Your role as a coach is to accompany the client in this reflection process, which at times may seem like a negotiation but ultimately is about finding the best outcomes for the children and their families.

Infants provide another example. In some cultures, caregivers believe it is fine to allow infants to cry and think that they may become spoiled if they are given too much attention when they cry. However, current research on child development has found it important to be highly responsive to infants' needs. This topic came up with one of my (Erika's) clients. The client was terribly upset about the idea of needing to respond every time infants cry. She was a family child care educator and had many children of different ages to care for. She said it would be impossible for her to stop whatever she was doing every single time to go to infants who cried. This prompted an authentic and respectful conversation about her experiences in her culture and country of origin surrounding child rearing, especially in infancy. The conversation explored how diverse cultures take different perspectives on it as well as the current research that has found how establishing positive attachments helps children build resilience from early on. We explored different possibilities for how she could be more responsive to infants' needs while also taking care of the other children of different ages, without being overwhelmed. Having this conversation about her beliefs about early childhood allowed us to truly go deep into it. With a transactional approach to coaching, the client may have just moved her head up and down and said, "Yes, you are right, you are right! I am going to do it," but then gone back to her usual responses when I left. By being culturally responsive, we connect with people's beliefs on a deeper level, strengthening relationships and propelling the sustainable long-term change process.

The Client's Goals

What are your client's goals? What are their *true* goals? Why did they choose the profession of early childhood education? What brought them here? Where do they see themselves in six months, one year, five years, ten years? How can you as a coach help your client get closer to their real goals?

These are very deep and relevant questions in coaching. Very possibly, the organization that hired you as a coach has certain learning goals and requirements they must meet as a program, and your job is to help specific stakeholders reach those goals. That is fantastic! From a systems perspective, we need certain parameters of standards to meet so we can advance the overall quality of care and education we are offering children. This is also relevant for funders of early childhood programs—governments, foundations, donors, and so on—that need to show the impact of the money they invest. However, while you are working to fulfill those systemic goals and needs, you are also helping your client meet their own deep, true, and authentic goals. The various goals do not have to be separated. They go hand in hand with your coaching relationship with the client.

Your client's goals are probably interconnected with their values. If we can have deep conversations with clients about their values, their goals, and how they are in concert with their professional role, we may advance much more deeply in our coaching relationship. We can seek correlations between the client's values and goals and the organization's. We may find that they are closely intertwined and make connections between both. On the other hand, we may find that they are not that interconnected. In those cases, it may be necessary to have deep, reflective conversations about your client's long-term goals and discuss any changes they need to make so their goals correlate better with their day-to-day life. For example, you may find that your client really wants to pursue a career in nursing, and their motivation to continue in the field of early childhood education is low. Having clarity surrounding the client's real goals can help achieve long-term growth or fuel changes in their career path, if needed, for their ultimate happiness and satisfaction.

The Client's Dreams

If a fairy godmother appeared and granted you three wishes, what would you ask for? Allow yourself the possibility that anything can come true. It can be so liberating to connect deeply to what we really want and what our true dreams are. By asking your client a question like this, you can help them connect in a deeper way with their dreams. You are shifting your coaching from being merely superficial to a deeper personal, authentic level. After your client has shared their three wishes, you can consider how their work in early childhood education connects or correlates with their true and authentic dreams.

Why not work together with your clients to help them achieve their deepest aspirations while at the same time increasing their competencies in their current roles in early childhood education? As we help them connect with their authentic dreams, we may help them be more joyful in improving and growing as professionals. The personal and professional dreams of your clients do not need to be separated. Actually, the more interconnected their goals are, the more motivation the client feels, and the more that long-lasting growth and change can happen. Do not be afraid to ask your clients their own three wishes!

The Client's Needs

At the beginning of each coaching session, check in genuinely with your client, especially seeking to discover any specific needs they have. So many of us walk around the world with unfulfilled needs we have been unable to communicate. This can lead to stress, tension, and anxiety, among other negative effects. If you look very deeply into any negative emotion, you often find that behind that negative emotion is an unfulfilled need.

To help your client advance in their work in early childhood, ask how they are feeling. What do they need to feel happier and more fulfilled in their work in the early childhood field? What needs do they have currently in their family or in any other area of their life? It is not that we are there to help fulfill those needs, but through our coaching relationship we can listen and recognize and truly feel empathy for the client's needs. As you listen with empathy, many clients will feel a release of tension. They will know you genuinely care about them. Then you may be able to continue talking about more specific things related to their role in early childhood education and how you can help them. Your conversation may be much more fruitful because you took the time to connect with your client's specific needs.

The Client's Strengths

So much of current society is based on giving or receiving feedback about weaknesses, dwelling on what one is not doing well, being self-deprecating, and overall focusing on the negative. This approach creates a lot of self-judgment and shame. A strength-based approach to coaching focuses on what the client can do well, building on that to reach the client's goals. Many of us are so used to focusing on the negative—maybe because of cultural traits—that when it is time to talk about our actual strengths, we have difficulty finding examples. A wonderful way to go deeper in your relationship with your client and to show cultural responsiveness is to dedicate coaching conversations to the strengths of your client. What do they do well? Where do they feel very competent? Where do you see them being highly competent? Give specific examples and feedback on how you see their strengths and how they connect to reaching their goals.

Talk about your client's strengths in terms of the cultural diversity and perspectives they offer to the field of early childhood education. Culture is an asset, not a deficiency. Having diverse cultures represented in early childhood allows us to add more perspectives that may help the field advance. It is time to bring more awareness to the dominant culture of a society instead of seeing it as a default and to talk about how nondominant cultures also are huge assets to the overall society. There is no need to feel ashamed because one is different or thinks differently than the dominant culture. Talk about these differences as well as similarities and highlight how their perspective can help improve the lives of the children and families the program supports. Support your client and see that these cultural variations can be strengths.

The Client's Cultural Responsiveness

Just as you are taking the time to hear your client's voice and learn about their culture and perspectives, you may invite your client to follow a similar process with the children, staff, families, or any other stakeholders they interact with. It involves encouraging your client to have in-depth conversations with other stakeholders, such as families, children, and coworkers, about their perspectives and beliefs about diverse cultures and any biases they may have.

There is nothing wrong with having open conversations about possible cultural biases. It is through conversations and awareness that we can start to shift the current cultural perspective and paradigm to a more integrated and equitable approach. Have conversations with your client about how well they know the families their program serves. What do they know about the families' histories, backgrounds, values, and cultures in general? How can they find out more? How could this process of deepening cultural responsiveness to other stakeholders help us reach the goals we have set for the program?

Share with your client the specific strategies you have been using to make yourself more culturally responsive to them to help them follow a similar process with the other stakeholders. For example, encourage your clients to be interested in and curious about other stakeholders' culture, to communicate that they value and respect their culture, to include more elements in the program that reflect the stakeholders' culture, to invite them to share about their culture with others in the program, and to contribute elements of their culture in a way that forms part of the new cultural identity of the program.

The Client's Perspectives on Equity

What does your client know about equity? Many people are at different stages of understanding and applying equity in their everyday professional and personal practices. You may want to ask the client how they understand the term *equity* and how it compares to *equality*. You may also want to talk about how they currently apply strategies that will help promote equity in their professional life. For example, discuss how they become aware of what supports specific children and their families need to reach their goals. Based on that understanding, ask how they offer the tools needed by the children and their families. Reflect on how they individualize instruction or communication to be equitable with that specific child or family.

Culture and cultural perspectives are ever moving, changing, and evolving. Open conversations about equity may play a role in a collective shift in our understanding as a society that moves us all toward a more equitable approach to our everyday life. It is okay to bring up topics like these that are uncomfortable but can bring these beautiful results. The idea is not to impose our own perspectives on equity but to find out where the client is in their understanding. We offer questions to help them think at an even deeper level about equity and why it is so important to apply in our work in early childhood education. Some ideas:

- What does equity mean to you?

- Why do you think equity would be relevant in early childhood education?

- How would the children benefit if you adopted practices that foster equity?

- How can you be aware of areas of inequity in the program?

- What ideas could bring more equity in those areas?

You can also talk about any experiences that they have had personally with a lack of equity or with discrimination. If a client does share moments when they were not treated with equity, it may be uncomfortable. We do not want to make people speak about things that they are not comfortable talking about. However, if they are open to it and we do have a strong relationship, talking about these painful times can deepen relationships, encourage emotional healing, and promote problem solving and actions for positive social change.

The Client's Perspective on Discrimination

One of the most powerful tools we have to be anti-discriminatory and anti-racist is to have more open dialogues on these topics. As we establish a strong relationship with our client, there may come a moment when we can have open conversations about racism and discrimination or talk about instances when they were personally discriminated against because of their identity. Diverse cultures have been put down or looked down on for many reasons—race, religion, beliefs, and a variety of other aspects. Having an open dialogue like this can inspire moments of reflection that we can then also connect to the client's experiences with the children and families in their program. As Paulo Freire said, sometimes we are oppressed and other times we are the oppressors. In his work in Brazil, he found that at the beginning of the twentieth century, farmworkers there were being oppressed, working extremely long hours for minimal pay. But through reflection the farmers also realized that they too were oppressing others below them, such as family members or other people in their community. In the same sense, Freire invites us to think about how we have been oppressed and at the same time who we oppress. Many times, oppressing others may come from a subconscious perspective. For example, sometimes oppression comes from cultural elements that we never questioned before but that have oppressing effects on others. For example, toddlerhood is one of the least understood stages of human development, and in a way, children at this age may be undergoing oppression. Think about how often we hear the cliché "terrible twos." Adults frequently feel they have to control toddlers, telling them what they can or cannot do. When this happens, toddlers often express their feelings of oppression with tantrums, which in turn may result in adults trying to exert more control, thus entering an endless cycle of oppression toward the child. In fact, toddlers are going through a developmental stage when they are learning independence. They are developing many language, cognitive, social-emotional, and motor skills, which combine with their interest in learning how to navigate in the world with autonomy. Adults can end this unconscious oppression toward toddlers by providing guidance to support the development of this autonomy instead of trying to control the child.

The more we have open conversations about discrimination and oppression, the more we can bring awareness and push for changes. Even if it is difficult in the beginning to talk about discrimination, it is necessary for us to continue moving forward as a global community.

Celebrating Your Client's Story

Your client's story has made them who they are today and will affect their future work in early childhood education. As a coach, you can come to truly appreciate your clients for who they are. Sometimes your client is quite different from you, with vastly different perspectives in political, religious, and ideological areas. But isn't it wonderful that we are a diverse society! We can keep society open by pursuing dialogue that helps us reach a deeper understanding of our humanity, realizing more similarities connect us than apparent differences divide us.

As you deepen your relationship with your client by being culturally responsive, you may find many interconnections. Build on those connections. Celebrate yourself and celebrate your client! And together through your collaboration you will be able to make a more aware, conscious, and thoughtful impact on future generations. Embrace it.

Revisit the reflective questions on page 45. How have your responses changed? How have they stayed the same?

Competencies

- Know your clients at a deep level.

- Understand your clients' culture.

- Connect with your clients.

- Be client-centered.

- Use knowledge of your clients to empower the change process.

- Engage in powerful conversations that support equity.

Practices

- Hear your client's story.

- Ask questions to deepen your understanding of your client.

- Learn about your client's professional goals.

- Learn about your client's personal goals.

- Anchor your coaching based on your client's goals.

- Learn about your client's heritage and family history.

- Know your client's essence: their interests, temperament traits, and learning styles.

- Know your client's perspectives on early childhood education.

- Listen to understand, not just respond.

Hear Your Client's Voice

- Tell me about you!

- What do you love?

- What makes you happy?

- What excites you about your work in early childhood education?

- Tell me about your family.

- What do you know about the heritage of the families you work with?

- Can you tell me a bit about your social identities?

- What are your top five values?

- Have you ever had a coach before? If so, can you share a bit about that experience?

Hear Your Voice

- What other strategies have worked for you to get to know your clients at a deeper level?

- Think about clients with whom you have developed deep relationships. What helped you develop those relationships?

References and Resources

Freire, Paulo. 2000. *Pedagogy of the Oppressed.* New York: Continuum.

Rosenberg, Marshall B. 1999. *Nonviolent Communication: A Language of Compassion.* Del Mar, CA: PuddleDancer Press.

Whitman, Walt. 1855. "Song of Myself." *Leaves of Grass.*

CHAPTER 4

Responding to Diverse Settings

People are people, and children are still children, no matter the setting.

Voices from the Field: Irma

Irma had worked with children for seven years before she joined the Quality Improvement Network. When she launched her business, she felt that all she needed to work with children was a Child Development Associate (CDA) credential, since that was all licensing required. Over the next seven years, Irma took the required training and felt that she knew all that she needed to be a successful caregiver. It wasn't until she joined a pilot quality improvement program that she realized she didn't know what she didn't know. Over the course of the five years of the program, Irma actively engaged with peers during professional learning sessions and continuously reflected on her journey with her coach's support.

She often reflected that she started her family child care business because it was the best option for her and her family. As a business owner, she learned how to manage licensing paperwork so her compliance monitor could easily find the documents she was looking for, thus reducing the burden on both of them. She was positively recognized by the government oversight organization for her well-organized files and willingness to comply with safety regulations. Yet she always felt undervalued compared to her center-based counterparts. She felt that yearly lesson plans and a larger group setting was perceived as learning, while her playful responsive interactions with infants and toddlers were "simply" caregiving. She was often referred to with, and accepted, the title of "babysitter," while her counterparts at centers were referred to as "teachers" by the families they served. And unlike her center-based colleagues who had opportunities to reflect and share their ideas with other adults and professionals, she often felt isolated, as she ran the administration, nutrition, education, and family engagement aspects of her business by herself.

It wasn't until she participated in the ongoing coaching and in the network that she understood and valued her significant role in the life of every child she interacted with. She learned to appreciate her natural ability to create open-ended toys with recycled materials that fostered children's critical thinking. Through the responsive coaching, she felt heard and understood, which in turn helped her understand herself at a deeper level. She also felt that others increasingly respected her home and ideas. Thanks to a culturally responsive coach and a network of other family child care owners, she finally felt connected to other professionals and colleagues.

Reflective Questions

- What is your experience working in different settings?

- How different are the organizational cultures in each setting? How do the beliefs and practices of each setting affect how you interact with your clients?

- How has the setting influenced how you build trusting relationships with your clients? How have these relationships contributed to understanding each setting and person?

- What is your experience working with or supporting others to work with different age groups?

- Do you feel more comfortable with or have more knowledge of a particular setting?

- Do you feel more comfortable with or have more knowledge of a particular age group?

- What terminology do you tend to use when referring to different settings, age groups, or adults working in each of these programs? Do you refer to them as teachers, educators, providers, babysitters? Or have you devised ways to emphasize their uniqueness and value?

- How do your clients feel about the setting and age group with which they work? Do they feel supported, valued, and treated as professionals?

- Have you explored a variety of strategies to support your clients in different settings and age groups?

This chapter highlights how culturally responsive coaching responds to and builds on the strengths of different program settings and children's age groups. We begin our conversation by remembering that the children, no matter the age or setting, are the ultimate stakeholders of a culturally responsive coaching process. We aim to draw you into a reflective conversation around the differences and similarities across varied early childhood settings while keeping in mind that no matter the setting, the ultimate goal is providing high-quality programming for all children. We explore each setting's nuances and how a culturally responsive coaching process mirrors and enhances quality in all settings and at all levels.

We explore how the different roles in center-based settings influence the center's quality and consider how to engage directors while supporting multiple teaching teams. Similarly, we delve into culturally responsive coaching in family child care settings, where one person often assumes a multitude of roles. Our conversation around family child care also considers how to establish a trusting relationship in a setting that is someone's home. We also present a brief overview of the values and practices that influence each setting, to highlight how a culturally responsive coaching process can lead to sustainable change. Through the reflective questions we present in this chapter, we offer you the opportunity to consider your own experiences with institutional and cultural requirements and think about how best to meet these demands without losing sight of the essence of your and your client's voices.

Keeping Children at the Forefront

Children are children, whether in a center, family child care, or family, friend, neighbor (FFN) setting. Thus, to support children in reaching their full potential, early childhood professionals need certain foundational knowledge, skills, and dispositions, no matter where they work or with whom. Topics common to all programs include understanding child development, following safety and health guidelines, setting up an engaging learning environment, working with families, and performing ongoing assessment. Likewise, early childhood professionals working with any age and setting need to know how to build responsive, trusting relationships with the families who entrust children to their care and education. They need to know what to do to respond to individual children and foster positive relationships with others. The professional early childhood educator needs to be a lifelong learner who is open to working on a team, learning from others, engaging in self-reflection, and being flexible when needed.

At any age, children need to be engaged in meaningful experiences that respond to their learning styles, interests, and family background. Access to developmentally appropriate materials is essential to foster learning, development, and overall well-being. Ongoing communication with families is vital to support children across all ages and settings. However, although the knowledge and components of a quality early childhood program cut across settings, the special considerations of their setting and the age group they serve influences what is covered and how culturally responsive coaching is implemented.

The setting and age of the children influence the program's values, beliefs, and practices. Quality may look different for an infant program in a center versus a family child care setting, yet the ultimate goal is to support children's innate drive to learn and build trusting relationships. Infants and toddlers need the loving guidance of an educator who follows their lead and expands upon it by carefully planning meaningful experiences. Programs that cater to older children who are developmentally ready to engage in self-directed exploration alone or with friends blossom with an educator who guides their exploration by asking open-ended questions that help children make their thinking process visible. As we engage with programs, we often hear statements from educators, supervisors, and families about values related to their different settings. Some families value a homelike setting and building a long-term relationship that includes multiple siblings. Other families look for a school setting that features more academic instruction. Others value the convenience of having a program near their home or workplace to make pickup and drop-off easier. These priorities influence their selection of the program and what their expectations are for the program's ongoing interactions with children and families. The following sections look further into how a culturally responsive coaching process adapts to each setting and age group.

Reflection

What values, practices, and beliefs have you seen that are similar across settings or age groups? Are there aspects of the setting, such as the environment or size of the group, that you have found are more suitable for infants, preschooler, or mixed-age groups? Which setting or age group are you most comfortable working in? Which align with the values, beliefs, and practices of your client and you? How can you bridge the misalignment if there is one?

Nomenclature Influences Perception

Words convey meaning in many ways beyond their technical definition. The value we place on a word influences our perception and behavior. In Spanish, for example, the place you take a child during the day is often referred to as the *guardería*, literally "a place to store children." In English, *babysitter* might be used for in-home settings. Think of the difference between these and words like *educator* or *teacher*. Even among early childhood professionals, *caregiver*, *educator*, and *teacher* are used for different settings, and each has a different value attached to it. A program called a *preschool* tends to be given more importance because it is focused on "school readiness." By the mere use of the term *caregiver* instead of *educator* in infant and toddler programs, they might not be given as much respect. Yet these professionals lay the foundation for the rest of the children's lives. A client who works in a family child care setting may have a different self-perception than a client who works in a program linked to a school or Head Start program. A client's self-perception could influence their interaction with the children, families, and coach. In turn, we coaches may be using different terms to refer to each client based on where they work, which can bring unconscious bias to our interaction.

CHANGING PERCEPTIONS

In 2016 the Office of the State Superintendent of Education (OSSE) in Washington, DC, increased its educational requirements for all early childhood staff working in center and home-based programs. Although these changes were aimed at increasing quality, the response from key stakeholders was met with mixed reactions. For example, some family child care owners and staff working with infants and toddlers responded with statements such as "We don't need to go to college to learn how to change diapers"; "I'm too old to go back to the classroom; my brain is rusty"; "I've been doing this for decades. I don't need to learn anything new that will be obsolete in a few years anyway." Their perception of the knowledge needed, the recognition of their job, and the role that they played in the lives of children was different from what was now being demanded. Up to now, they had been valued by how well they complied with safety and health regulations, not for their contributions to setting the foundation for the learning and development of the children in their program. With ongoing support from universities, community-based organizations and foundations, and government agencies, there is increased awareness of and support for their critical contribution and the extensive knowledge and skills that are required to be the architect of a child's future.

Building on the Strengths of Different Settings

Early childhood comprises a myriad of programs and settings that serve young children and their families. Some of these are more readily available to different populations than others due to funding, enrollment processes, family preferences, and hours of operation. We begin to explore how a culturally responsive coaching process can build on each setting's strengths by understanding and engaging with their differences. This, in turn, contributes to the optimal learning, support, and overall well-being of your client.

In-home settings: Family, friend, and neighbor (FNN) and family child care (FCC)

Home-based programs encompass a variety of situations, whether they are licensed, regulated, or not registered with any regulatory agency, and whether the owner's children attend. These settings fall under the category of family child care (FCC) programs and are referred to as child development homes; family day homes; and family, friend, and neighbor (FFN) care. The information and strategies presented here are primarily geared to FCC programs in which families pay for their children to be taken care of in another person's home and are part of a formal support system that has contracted you as their coach. Although FFN is not discussed in depth in this section, understanding why they started, who supports them, how they work with children and families, and how to build on their strengths is essential to a culturally responsive coaching approach. FFN settings are defined by many states as informal, unregulated child care offered for children of family members or neighbors. It is informal in that there may or may not be a contract, and in some cases there is no financial exchange. The person caring for the child is a trusted family member or neighbor who provides services that respond to the unique needs of the family. As they tend to be unregulated, many fall under the radar of licensing agencies that ensure compliance with safety, health, and quality regulations. Regardless, they offer an important service to families who need care for their children while they work. Although there is limited information comparing the types of settings, government agencies and funders are paying more attention to how to support the adults in FFN to ensure that *all* children, no matter the setting, have a quality early childhood experience.

FCC arrangements often begin when a parent or close relative stays home with their child and then begins caring for other children alongside. Various reasons can prompt this decision, including the economic situation or the belief that their children are better cared for at home. The space where the children and adults spend most of their day can be an integral part of the home, such as a living or dining room, or can be located in a separate room specifically set aside for the purpose of the FCC.

The family situation, their reasons for opening their homes to others, and their existing support systems influence the relationships educators have with their coaches. For example, if you were sent into the FFC to coach an educator because of their low scores on a standardized assessment tool, they may already be resistant to change because they associate it with compliance issues. On the other hand, if the educator is part of a supported cohort and everyone has an assigned coach, they will likely feel more open to learn and share. Regardless of the individual circumstances, it is vital to remember that you are entering into someone's home. It is much more than a child care business; a family lives there. At the end of the day, your client does not shut the door to go home; they are home.

If you have worked with FCC educators, you know they take on multiple roles in starting, managing, and running an early childhood program. They wear the hat of a business owner as they track their finances and handle the administrative tasks of ordering, contracting, and managing a business. Your client also wears the educator's hat, working directly with children or serving as a supervisor if the program is large enough to hire staff. At times they also wear a nutritionist's hat, if they are serving food or are part of a regulated food program. Family engagement and social work are essential duties added to your client's hat rack as they enroll and support families in their program. Many FCC clients build relationships with families over an extended time period as they serve younger siblings.

The public at large may perceive FCCs as profit-making businesses. However, when you consider the ten-to-twelve-hour days that many FCCs are open, along with cost of benefits such as time off and health insurance, the income may barely cover expenses. In some cases, family members end up subsidizing the cost of running the business, leaving little left over to put into retirement or a savings account. Despite these challenging operational conditions, the commitment and deep relationships they build with their families motivates these small businesses forward.

Consider whether your FCC client is a regulated or nonregulated FCC program. This does not necessarily affect the program's quality, but it does influence which entities your client is beholden to. For example, regulations that govern FCC licensing and operation vary from place to place and are dependent on local, state, and federal requirements. Some may not have a license to operate, either because of the number of children they serve or because licensing demands and support are too cumbersome or perceived as unrealistic. Your client might be part of the increased effort in several states to bring these programs into quality improvement initiatives.

Work to gain an understanding of any variations or contradictions that exist between licensing requirements and quality initiatives. For example, the number of adults per child requirements that are specified in the licensing regulations may be different from what is essential for responsive interactions. Various entities' requirements may also be at odds with each other, which in turn produces stress and confusion for your client. Offices that manage subsidy programs might have their own forms for taking attendance while the Department of Health or the Office of Head Start might have other forms for similar purposes. Having more knowledge about the slew of actors that influence the day-to-day management of your client's FCC will contribute to understanding their perspective, determine who to reach out to for additional support and networking, and help connect the dots. With a holistic approach that takes into account not only the learning components but also the business side of financing, regulations, and resources, you are better able to serve your client. That doesn't mean that you will be working in all of these areas; it does mean that you are better equipped to be empathetic and understand the many facets of their role.

There may be many instances when the language you speak is not the same as your FCC clients, especially if they speak a language that is not widely used in your area and no coach who speaks their language is available. The language your client speaks does not determine their commitment to providing a quality program. What may affect your client's quality and your relationship is how easily communication flows. Speaking the same language builds a sense of trust and understanding that contributes to sustainable change. A different energy level exists when thoughts and feelings are shared with someone who speaks the same language.

When you don't speak the same language, it's critical to listen to your client's voice through alternative forms of communication, such as interpreters or electronic translation platforms. If using interpreters, you may want to get to know one or two whom an organization uses on a regular basis and with whom your client feels comfortable. This helps with consistency and contributes to working as a team. Schedule extra time for the call so your client does not feel rushed. It takes much longer to say the same thing when it has to be repeated in different languages. Another strategy that works well is running the notes from your conversation through an online translation platform during the session. It's so exciting to see your client recognize their words in their language! Take caution using this technology with clients whose literacy level in their own language is not fluid.

Reflection

Have you had clients who are FCC owners or educators? Do you know what prompted them to open their homes to children and families? What are their successes and challenges? Which entities regulate their operation? How are their values, beliefs, and practices aligned with those of the regulatory agencies?

A culturally responsive coaching approach must consider the places where children in FCC settings are cared for and engaged throughout the day. Environment facilitates behavior, and knowing where activities occur and how connected they are to your client's family will help you understand their values, beliefs, and practices. Setting may influence children's interactions, behavior, learning experience, and relationships with other family members.

The experiences and activities that your client provides likely need to respond to the developmental level and interest of a mixed-age group, and the daily routine must include diaper changing, block building, art activities, reading, and individual and large-group activities. As you work with your client around implementing curriculum, you need to understand the setting's influence and how it can be used to enhance learning for a wide age range of children, sometimes from a few months old to school age. For example, older children can get comfy on a couch while you sit on the floor with infants as they crawl on your lap. The older children feel even bigger in a new space they can now climb onto, while the infant feels your nearness and is secure to explore their environment.

An important component of a quality program is setting up a process of collecting information that will help your client make meaningful decisions, along with taking stock of the quality of their program and the development of the children. This data collection takes place at different levels. For example, observations of the children can be used to better understand a particular child, which allows responsive planning to support that child's learning and development. At the environment level, educators can collect information on how to optimize the use of their space (or have someone else come and collect it for them).

A slew of tools is available to gather this information in an FCC setting. There are simple tools, such as Deb Curtis and Margie Carter's book *Designs for Living*, that educators use to reflect on how responsive the environment is for infants, toddlers, and preschoolers. Likewise, there are standardized tools administered by trained observers. However, these tools become moot if the data they collect is not aligned with the culture of the children and your client or if the results cannot easily be used. For example, if your client merges their program space with the family space in a small living room, it may not be practical to have separate learning centers that have to be set up and taken down every day. Instead, it may be easier—and better woven into the learning experience—to have boxes with materials that are brought out at different moments of the day and then tucked back into a corner with children's assistance. Having a tool that tells your client that they are out of compliance for not having learning centers visible may create more resistance and stifle learning. On the other hand, gathering information on their space and working with your client to identify the best way to keep children healthy and safe, while fostering learning and connections, will be more productive.

To be effective, any coaching approach needs to include undivided time with your client to build a relationship, reflect, plan, and follow up on agreed-upon action items. However, in an FCC, finding the time when your client can give you their undivided attention when they barely have the chance to take a break is challenging. It is under these circumstances that a culturally responsive approach is essential and flexibility a must. Naptime, evenings, and even Saturdays may be the only moments when they can take the time for this vital reflection. Finding creative ways to set aside this time and work with your client will lead to meaningful and productive conversations.

Center-based programs

Center-based programs serve a large group of children, typically separated by age group with staff assigned to each group. Centers range in size from one room to multiple classes across many sites. They also vary in their mission and programming. For example, some run out of a church and offer a half-day program. Other centers are situated in a school, under a principal and education coordinator's jurisdiction, while yet others are part of a national Head Start program. Profit-based centers have become more common since the 1980s, as has employee-sponsored early childhood care. Access to resources and support will vary considerably within the different types of centers. Funding can come from families, organizations, and governmental and nongovernmental institutions associated with a variety of regulatory agencies, which influence the center's values, beliefs, and practices. If the organization is part of a government-funded program, the practices will be driven by the funders' regulations. Centers affiliated with Head Start programs are governed by the Head Start Performance Standards, while privately run centers are regulated by local licensing or organizational structures. An organization's values and beliefs may also drive its structure, interactions with families, and the setup of the environment. An organization that prioritizes working with families alongside their children may structure its program so that it caters to both audiences. All of these variations can influence your coach-client relationship.

An educator working in a center interacts with colleagues and supervisors, and these interactions influence the outcome of the coaching process. Center-based programs create a community of learners for teachers across their classrooms, which can elevate the level of peer-to-peer learning and improve the care they provide. An educator who has a responsive support system will need a different type of coaching than someone who is at odds or not aligned with the organization's or teammates' culture. During the initial phase of the coaching process, an important step is to take stock of who the other adults in the organization are and how they influence your client's professional learning. This will contribute to a holistic and systemic approach. This joint exploration and reflection could include responding to the following questions:

- Which other actors influence what happens in the center?

- What are their roles, and how do they support your client?

- What is the relationship between your client and the other actors?

For example, if your client is the lead teacher, what are their responsibilities to plan and to complete administrative tasks versus those of other adults in the program? Do they work as coteachers, or does one supervise the others? If your client is a supervisor, what is their relationship with the teachers, or what is their perceived role in relation to the people they supervise? In some cases, especially in small programs, the lead teacher also might be the director or education coordinator. Since your client has the dual role of teacher and supervisor due to the small size of the program, coaching your client in how to support their teachers will deepen their own understanding at the same time. They aren't just learning it for themselves in their role as a teacher; they need to know it at a deeper level to support the teachers they supervise.

INCREASING RESPONSIVE CURRICULUM:
Reflections from a Coach in a Center-Based Program

During one of our coaching sessions, my client expressed her frustration at not being able to implement a responsive approach with the infants and toddlers in her classroom. As a teacher's assistant, she felt the lead teacher's curriculum was static and prescriptive. When she tried to share with her colleague her observations of a child and how it helped her understand their development, the response she got included comments such as, "That's nice, but we don't have time to respond to each child as an individual. The curriculum lays out the activities, and all we have to do is follow it." During our coaching sessions, we explored how to respond to meet her colleagues where they were. We looked at strategies to use her observations to work with children within the curriculum in the meantime.

How a Culturally Responsive Coaching Approach Serves Unique Populations

Early childhood programs cater to families from diverse backgrounds and situations. Young children are dependent on their families and do not have a say in where or how they live. Supporting your client to observe children to see them as individuals and understand what they are trying to figure out in the world will contribute to a responsive learning environment, no matter their circumstances. Being aware of your mannerisms, tone of voice, and facial expressions will help communicate your respect and curiosity to learn. As you work with your client and build empathy for the families' unique circumstances, encourage your client to reflect on their own childhood experiences of schooling and child-rearing practices. These memories will enhance their understanding of how their cultural beliefs influence how they work with children of different ages, backgrounds, and development levels. Similarly, gathering information from families about their child-rearing practices and their understanding of child development will foster a much-needed partnership. The analysis of this information will help your client respond to each child's individual qualities and support families as their child's first and foremost teacher.

Working with refugee families

When coaching and supporting staff from programs that enroll children and families who arrived in the United States as refugees, there are additional factors to consider surrounding the families themselves and the support mechanisms available for their transition to a new country, culture, and life. Counsel your client to build trusting relationships by working to understand the circumstances that led the families to seek refuge in the United States. It may be difficult for some families to share their experiences, especially if they have been traumatic. The following reflective, relationship-building questions will help you to guide your client and support them to reflect on these issues and respond accordingly.

- What are the family's dreams and aspirations for their children?

- How similar or different were the children's activities in their home country?

- What was the educational situation in their home country, such as availability of resources, access to child care, and program policies?

- What level of education did parents attain? Are they in the process of continuing their education?

- Did children witness or experience trauma? If so, when and for how long?

- Are child-rearing practices similar or different in their home country?

The purpose of these questions is to build a relationship with the families and gain knowledge that will help you and your client show empathy and respect. These questions will also mirror for your client the importance of sharing this information in a culturally responsive coaching process.

Reflection

What experience do you have working with programs that cater to refugee populations? What is your understanding of the lives they left and their reasons for coming to the United States? Are you aware of any filters that influence how you perceive programs that enroll children and families who are refugees? How does your perception of refugees affect how you support your clients?

Working with dual-generation programs

Dual-generation programs offer a unique opportunity for the educational, social, and health needs of the adults and children in a family to be addressed in the same program. In these programs, adult members of the family continue their education, often taking classes in English, technology, or a particular certification. Children of the adult students enroll in programs and activities while their parents are in class. As these programs cater to adults and children, understanding curriculum strategies for adult learning and children is helpful. Although you may be coaching the teachers of young children, they will in turn be working more closely with the families as an integral part of the program.

Although the program strategies are different for adults and for children, there may be opportunities for cross-pollination. For example, parents might be offered classes in child development as part of their English lessons and also spend time in the classroom with their child learning how to support their development.

RESPONDING TO THE COVID-19 PANDEMIC

Briya Public Charter School, founded in 1989, is a dual-generation program that serves adults and children of families from diverse backgrounds. It has vast experience in being intentional in responding to the evolving needs of both adults and children. To ensure the quality of their services, Briya has coordinators who work directly with the teachers and meet on a monthly basis to coach them. As the COVID-19 pandemic hit in 2020, their usual in-person activities had to adapt quickly to an online platform. The coordinators and teachers met virtually to figure out new strategies to continue their mission while keeping everyone safe. Since they no longer could have classes in person and many of the teachers and families did not have access to a computer, the coordinators devised a plan to provide staff and families with the computers they normally used for testing. At the start of the COVID pandemic, Briya's staff had to grapple with uncertainty in terms of how long the early childhood and adult education classes were going to be held virtually and how to protect families' and staff's health as they picked up computers or materials from the centers. The coordinators, in their coaching role, met with the early childhood staff each week to adapt the curriculum so that families became the teachers of their children. They shifted to engaging parents directly and sharing activities that adults could replicate with their children. It was thanks to the trusting relationship that the team, including the coaches, had built with the families and children that the transition from in-person to this novel way of working was successful.

Tailoring the work to different age groups and developmental levels

Children are children, regardless of the early childhood setting. However, they each have individual needs, they grow and develop at different rates, and they interact with their surroundings in distinctive ways. Regardless of the setting where your client works, understanding their values, beliefs, and practices and their knowledge and skills for working with a particular age group of children is essential to achieving positive outcomes. For example, do you know your client's understanding of the unique developmental levels, temperaments, and needs of the children they serve? Have they had more experience with an older age group and are adapting to younger children? Are the curriculum guidelines your client needs to implement aligned with the children's developmental needs?

An important quality element in programs serving infants and toddlers, for example, is the practice of continuity of care. This happens when a child has the same educator over an extended period, sometimes from birth until they transition into preschool. This of course is a challenge when there is a high turnover rate in a program. Unlike programs that transition children from one educator to another when they reach specific milestones, ideally continuity of care allows children to establish a trusting relationship with one person over time. It lets educators get to know the children and families and provide consistent guidance to enhance their learning and development. However, this quality component requires educators to understand the needs of children during a time of rapidly changing growth and development. These needs cut across health, safety, and emotional and learning areas. Support your client's understanding that learning happens through the infants' and toddlers' daily routines and that large-group and academic-focused activities only stifle that learning process. Focusing on the daily routines will also support your clients in being responsive to the health and safety needs of children.

Reflection

What is your vision of infants and toddlers? How can you help clients feel awe in infants' and toddlers' innate capacity to learn and their desire for relationships? How can you support your clients to understand the interconnection between health, nutrition, and learning in everyday interactions?

Your clients who work with preschool-age children likewise need to build trusting relationships and engage in meaningful experiences with children and families. However, the focus is more on social interactions, learning, and guiding behavior. You may work with your client to understand the cultural nuances of what school readiness means in different contexts and align these with the setting in which they work. For example, an early childhood setting may interpret school readiness to mean teaching children the alphabet and reading and writing, in contrast to a more holistic understanding of school readiness that encompasses skills and behaviors related to problem solving, self-regulation, and adaptability.

Reflection

What is your experience working with preschool children? How do you use this information to reflect on your and your client's values, beliefs, and practices related to school readiness? How do you support your clients to engage in meaningful conversations with families to gather and use information that supports their child to reach their full potential?

Revisit the questions on page 62. How have your responses changed? How have they stayed the same?

Competencies

- Be aware of your knowledge and preferences regarding different settings so you can be responsive to all clients, no matter where or with whom you work.

- Focus on the child as the ultimate reason for your coaching sessions and reinforce the essential role your clients play in children's overall learning and well-being.

- Respect and build on each setting's strengths to better hear all voices and foster optimal learning for all children.

- Approach data differently for each setting to ensure that the information you gather is meaningful and reflective of the setting.

Hear Your Client's Voice

- What knowledge presented in this chapter reinforces your coaching practices in different settings?

- What information is new or something you hadn't considered before?

- What new ways will you engage with your clients that respond best to their unique setting or age group?

Hear Your Voice

- How will you make your voice heard as you work with different institutional cultures?

- Do you feel a preference for one type of setting over others, and how can you use that awareness to mitigate potential differences, no matter the early childhood environment in which your clients work?

Hear Other Stakeholders

- Whose voices do you search out to better understand the individual characteristics of each setting?

- How can you incorporate their voices to support you and your client working in different settings?

References and Resources

BUILD Initiative. www.buildinitiative.org/Resources/Resource-Center.

ChildCare.gov. n.d. "Family Friend and Neighbor (FFN) Care." https://childcare.gov /index.php/consumer-education/family-friend-and-neighbor-care.

Childhood Education International. https://ceinternational1892.org.

Curtis, Deb, and Margie Carter. 2015. *Designs for Living: Transforming Early Learning Environments*, 2nd ed. St. Paul, MN: Redleaf Press.

Early Learning Challenge Technical Assistance. 2017. "Supports for Family, Friend, and Neighbor Child Care Providers in Early Learning Challenge States." https://files.eric .ed.gov/fulltext/ED583878.pdf.

Fidazzo, Gina, Laura Schmidt, and Alisia Bergsman. Bridging Refugee Youth and Children's Services. 2006. "Enhancing Child Care for Refugee Self-Sufficiency: A Training Resource and Toolkit." https://brycs.org/wp-content/uploads/2006/08 /EnhancingChildCare.pdf.

Head Start Early Childhood Learning and Knowledge Center. https://eclkc.ohs.acf.hhs .gov.

King, Christopher, Robert Glover, and Tara Smith. 2012. "Dual-Generation Strategy Initiative Research Brief." www.fcd-us.org/dual-generation-strategy-initiative -research-brief.

National Association for the Education of Young Children (NAEYC). www.naeyc.org.

National Association for Family Child Care (NAFCC). www.nafcc.org.

Program for Infant Toddler Care, WestEd. www.pitc.org.

Zero to Three. www.zerotothree.org.

CHAPTER 5

Coaching to Support Cultural Responsiveness and Equity

One cannot expect positive results from an educational or political action program which fails to respect the particular view of the world held by the people. Such a program constitutes cultural invasion, good intentions notwithstanding.

—Paulo Freire, *Pedagogy of the Oppressed*

Voices from the Field: Susanna

Susanna was given the caseload of clients she would be coaching for the school year. As she drove through the traffic of that autumn morning through her large metropolitan city, Susanna was thinking about how excited she was about meeting her new client. She had never been to this particular school and was curious about it because it was set in a remarkably diverse neighborhood in the city. Susanna thought this would be a fantastic opportunity to work with different community backgrounds through her coaching.

After parking her car in the large parking lot, she walked through the main entrance, signed in at the main office, and was then guided through the long halls to reach the room where she was to meet her new client, Maria. Maria was notified that her coach was waiting for her in the conference room. Five minutes, ten minutes, fifteen minutes passed, and no sign of Maria. Susanna went to the main office again to inquire if there had been any change in the program or agenda since Maria had not shown up yet. The office assistant said she was not aware of any changes, and she would again go and check in with Maria to remind her that her coach was waiting in her conference room.

Susanna sat down again in the conference room. She jotted down some additional notes on her coach planning form as she waited. Susanna was very well versed in relationship building and getting to know her clients. When Maria finally arrived, Susanna showed her natural positive disposition, frequently smiling and behaving in a warm and friendly manner toward Maria. However, Maria just sat with her arms crossed.

"I do not want you to be my coach," Maria said in a negative tone. Susanna was surprised to see such negativity. She tried to inquire a little bit more into her comment.

"I am tired of people who do not look like me coming to tell me what to do." As Maria said this, she was pointing to her skin. Maria asserted that this was a waste of her time and she was not willing to embark on such a process again with another coach. This was a huge shock to Susanna. What kind of experiences had Maria gone through?

Susanna wanted to be very respectful toward Maria. She tried to put herself in her client's shoes. Susanna could tell that Maria had had adverse or even traumatic experiences with previous coaches or mentors. Susanna told Maria that she respected her views and would see what could be done to provide her with a mentor with whom she would be comfortable.

Maria was surprised that Susanna had actually heard and responded to her frustration. Susanna asked Maria if she could just ask her a question. She asked if she had had previous difficult experiences with coaches that brought her to feel this way. Maria started sharing experiences she'd had with her previous coach, who would always come and tell her everything that was wrong with her without listening to her. That coach used only assessment data, trying to prod her to get better scores. Maria also mentioned that her previous coach made several comments she felt were discriminatory and made her feel extremely uncomfortable. Maria mentioned that as a Black woman from Dominican Republic, she felt that the previous coach could not understand her heritage nor who she was as a human being.

Well, it turned out that Susanna herself was from a nearby country in the Caribbean and had visited Maria's country once. Susanna mentioned that her boyfriend was also Black and from the Caribbean. They started chatting about places in town they loved to go to listen to Caribbean music as well as other cultural connections. They also spoke about how it feels to be Latinas in the United States. They both shared a passion for social justice and saw education as a way to bring more equity to society. By recognizing these connections and similarities, Maria opened up to the possibility of a coaching relationship.

From this very rough start, Susanna was able to establish the foundations of a strong relationship. It did not come out of nowhere. Susanna had previously taken the time to know herself, including her own family's cultural heritage. She took the time to learn about Maria, her history and culture, and her needs. Through the following coaching sessions, they were able to deepen their relationship, and skin color was no longer an obstacle. Susanna built into their coaching goals Maria's passion for building more equitable systems in her classroom. Long-term equitable change was taking place. It was a constructive and successful coaching year.

By taking the time to learn more about your client, you may find that you have more similarities than you thought, despite any cultural differences. By highlighting similarities, you can connect more deeply with your client and help this to be a strength in the coaching relationship.

Reflective Questions

- What does equity mean to you?

- What is the difference between short-term and long-term change in coaching for early childhood professionals?

- What role does cultural responsiveness play in supporting equity?

- Have you ever seen cultural biases or inequities in the programs where your clients work?

- How could your coaching help promote equity to your clients?

- Have your clients ever voiced inequities? If so, how have you responded?

- How can you help your clients feel empowered so their voices are heard in the field of early childhood?

Culturally responsive coaching can be a powerful tool to support equity in the field of early childhood. As we have explored in previous chapters, when we connect with the client's culture and our own culture, we go deeper into the relationship, which in turn can help achieve long-term change. We must also venture to have reflective conversations about how some aspects of our own culture could be limiting us in terms of taking new stances or building new understandings of the world. Some things about our culture can help us reach our aims. But at the same time, some things about our own culture may be getting in our way.

This chapter presents information and strategies for increasing your awareness of cultural and linguistic diversity for both you and your clients. It takes a deeper look at the factors that contribute to open communication and increase our ability to hear one another's voices. The information and strategies will facilitate self-reflection surrounding your and your client's biases and suggest ways to address these biases to achieve respect and understanding that leads to sustainable change. In addition, the chapter explores how coaching can help support equity.

Being an Equitable Coach

As mentioned in chapter 1, cultures evolve according to the societal needs of their present moment. Culture is not stagnant but fully alive and completely changing and evolving according to values, needs, and the times. Throughout the history of humanity, there have always been competing cultures, and unfortunately many injustices have come out of these clashes. One reason for these conflicts may be because individual human beings generally think that opposing or different perspectives are wrong and their own perspectives are true and better than others. These entrenched ways of thinking have brought much suffering for humanity. Even today most of us think that our own ideas are the truth and the most important ones. If somebody thinks differently from you, the natural tendency is to believe that they are wrong. But in the meantime, others are thinking the same thing about you! They have their own beliefs and ideas, and if they differ from you, they probably believe you are wrong.

There have been efforts throughout history to change these patterns and bring more justice and well-being to humanity. For example, in the 1960s the civil rights movement in the United States helped increase awareness and bring a deeper understanding that we all are equal: nobody is better than anyone else, and each person should have access to equal opportunities. This paradigm proved useful up to a certain point. Now as a society we realize that not everyone is born into equal circumstances, and some are born into circumstances that are far more difficult than others. Therefore, to fully support a child who is born in those different circumstances requires different resources. This is where equity comes in. Some people need more support than others or need support in different areas.

You cannot assume that following the same coaching format will meet the needs of every client. To be equitable as a coach means meeting the clients exactly where they are and finding out where they want to go, then helping provide resources so the client can get there. Therefore, each coaching session may look quite different. To have long-term sustainable change, we need to take this equitable stance.

Equitable Does Not Mean "Easier"

An interesting mistake we sometimes make is thinking that if a person faces a certain disadvantage, we need to make things easier for them. But that is the wrong mindset: it is not that we are making something easier but that we are providing the tools clients need to reach their goals. Indeed, using these tools may require more effort to reach the same goal, regardless of their circumstances. For example, there was once an initiative to do remote coaching for teachers in rural areas. The teachers had little knowledge of computer technology but were extremely interested in receiving coaching. The coaching team knew that technology would be an obstacle, so they made extra effort to provide one-on-one time with each teacher to help them learn how to turn on a computer, open an email account, respond to an email, and so on. It took more time and more effort for both the coaches and the teachers. However, it was needed to provide this support for these teachers so that they would be able to benefit from working one-on-one remotely with a coach. They also learned how to use other forms of technology, such as communicating with faraway family members using the internet. This coaching helped them move forward as human beings and as professionals in the field of early childhood education.

Equitable coaching isn't about making it "easy" for clients but rather offering what they need to reach their fullest potential and goals. Through intentional questioning, you help guide the client to find possible solutions or resources to fulfill their need. Support and advocate for clients as they implement steps to reach their goals. Celebrate success as your client gets closer to those goals.

Cultural Responsiveness and the Dominant Culture

The coaching process is strengthened when you venture into deeper conversations about the dominant culture. A dominant culture exerts control in a certain organization, region, or country during a specific period of time. We cannot overgeneralize cultures, but there are certain traits or tendencies that generally prevail in a dominant culture, such as the belief that it is better or more right than other cultures. These general traits of the dominant culture affect society as a whole. For example, in the United States the main dominant culture has been of white European origin. Unfortunately, white supremacy permeates many systems in the United States. When we take a deeper look into the current climate in the country, we see many examples of this white dominant culture at many scales.

Dominant culture affects the kind of questions we ask ourselves as we design research studies and thus affects the answers we get, including research in early childhood education. Unfortunately, the dominant culture's perspectives about designing, theorizing, and developing research has led to misconceptions. For example, some studies prior to the 1980s supposedly found that it was not to the child's advantage to develop as multilingual. But current research has found that being multilingual has vast benefits (Bialystok 2011). To break the paradigm that promoted monolingualism, diverse voices had to speak up and question the dominant culture, offering practical solutions from another cultural perspective. As more diverse voices join the research, we may be able to break through some of the limitations of the dominant culture.

White supremacy in the United States is not the only obstacle in moving toward an equitable world. Each country has its own dominant culture that can be an obstacle toward equity. For example, in Mexico the dominant culture is mestizo (a mix of European and indigenous descent), Christian, and middle/upper-middle social economic class. Their values dominate many systems in the country. You may hear someone from the dominant Mexican culture say, "We don't have diversity in Mexico; we are all Mexicans." However, this is not the case. There are many indigenous communities in Mexico as well as immigrants from other countries and communities with a variety of religious backgrounds, such as Jewish, Muslim, and so on. Sometimes people from the dominant culture may be blind to seeing diverse perspectives even within their own community. Racism, classism, and other forms of discrimination exist, even in developing countries. By becoming more aware of the dominant culture and talking about it during coaching sessions, we can bring more awareness to values that the dominant culture may be imposing and see whether they are interconnected with the actual values and goals of your client and the families with whom they work.

Speaking about the dominant culture is not about blaming or pointing fingers. It is about reflection. It is not about destroying what already exists but proposing new perspectives and solutions that may work even better, in a constructive and harmonious way. Remember that at times we may be oppressed, but in other circumstances we may be the oppressor. So taking time to see how you may be imposing your culture on others may also open the dialogue. For example, in a preschool classroom sometimes the teacher's culture dominates over the children's preferences and perspectives. Think about or talk with the children. Ask them about the daily routines and learning experiences and what they might like to do differently. When the teacher also offers ideas and has an open dialogue with the children, they can co-construct a classroom culture together that is inclusive from different perspectives. In the same way, through your coaching you can offer reflective questions about the dominant culture and establish an open dialogue that may help recognize voices that are not being heard and incorporate perspectives not only based on the dominant culture. You can help your client build up the confidence to be an active agent of positive change in society.

Coaching and Anti-Racism

We know that historically racism has brought hugely negative consequences to society. Racism has created hate, separation, injustice, trauma, and many other ills. Taking a passive stance toward racism does not help forward the goal of ending it: you must take an active role to be anti-racist. Racism can happen in a very unconscious way. Some people may not even notice that they are discriminating against others because of their race because it is so ingrained in their cultural belief systems that it just happens automatically. Many of these racist perspectives are transferred to children from an early age. Just think about the messages the media sends to young children about what is beautiful or good. For years cartoons and other media for young children have portrayed the dominant white culture in the United States as the desirable way to be. At the same time, by omitting nondominant cultures, the media sent the message that they were not desirable or acceptable. When children do not see themselves reflected in their environment, they may think there is something wrong with them.

Ask your client questions about culturally responsive practices that are being implemented in their program at various levels, and identify any areas that may be discriminatory. For example, ask how families of different cultures and languages are being included in the decision-making processes of the program. Are all the materials being translated to the families' languages to make sure they fully understand all communications? Are children and/or their families being treated differently because of their race and/or ethnicity? If so, how? Try to have intentional conversations about staff or coworkers, families, and children's cultures. Talk about the current practices your clients are following to be culturally responsive and brainstorm ideas about how they could be increased.

Coaching as an Agent of Change

Early childhood coaches are often hired because of an initiative to push change or growth in a certain area, such as improving the environment or teacher interactions, implementing a curriculum, and so on. However, in addition to any other goals or initiatives, you as the coach have the opportunity to explore how your client can infuse equity into their everyday work. For example, you can ask the client whether they see any areas where there is inequity. Do they have the resources to communicate with all the families in their program, even if nobody else in the program speaks the language? Are they able to communicate openly with all the families about their needs? If the answer is no, then there is an opportunity to investigate how they might create more equity for the affected families.

Some programs may think that because they have a bilingual Spanish-English speaker, they have all the needed resources in place for multilingual learners. However, what happens when there are children and families from less prevalent languages and cultures? How intentional is the program in providing equitable support to each family? You will often hear clients resist, asking, "How am I supposed to be able to have an interpreter for every language? How am I supposed to find the time to place labels across my classroom or learn key words in all those languages?" These are authentic questions; however, being equitable requires us to find resources to meet the needs of every family. Be creative to find out-of-the-box solutions together. Seek community nonprofit organizations that offer the services or support, or look for volunteers from family members or others in the community. Consider ways to raise funds for a specific need or reach out to government representatives for support.

For example, imagine that you are supporting a bilingual teacher in a pre-K classroom who works with families that speak Spanish and English. Now, a new child has enrolled in the program; he and his family have just immigrated to the United States from Korea. To be equitable, the program needs to invest the necessary resources to communicate and support the child and family. As a coach, you can ask who the translator and interpreter are and whether the program is translating all communications to the family. Does the program have an interpreter to come along on a home visit or for spontaneous communication? And so on. You may be able to find through this questioning a way to help the teacher think about creating more equity in the program. Asking questions from a strength-based approach, based on your strong relationship with your client, is most effective in creating sustainable change.

A lot of instances of racism or inequities are not performed at a conscious level. Sometimes reflective questioning and conversations can shine light in unseen areas if you have a strong relationship with your client in which both you and the client can be open and vulnerable. As a coach, you may also find that you have subconscious biases toward certain social identities. Allow yourself to go through this vulnerable process to learn from your clients and others, and to grow.

Strategies to Support Cultural Responsiveness and Equity

One of the first steps in supporting cultural responsiveness and equity as a coach is to know yourself at a deeper level, as we outlined in chapter 2. Think about your own culture, your own values, and your own history, which has brought you to where you are today. Allow yourself to be vulnerable to exploring any prejudices or biases toward other cultures or societal groups. It may be that biases were given to you through your family or the communities in which you grew up. Take the time to reflect on those biases and how having them is not helpful in our society. For example, you may want to write in a journal ideas that your family or community instilled in you regarding certain cultural groups. Were those perspectives biased? You may want to write about your real direct experiences with people of these cultural groups. Were your experiences different from the expectations or beliefs that were instilled in you? Try having open conversations with someone you trust about these experiences. You may even want to have a direct conversation with a person in that cultural group to learn more about them, and perhaps those prejudices may be dispelled. Further, you may consider taking an implicit bias test to gain a deeper understanding of possible biases that you may be unaware of.

Then, as outlined in chapter 3, take the time to have deep conversations with clients about their own culture and their own possible biases toward other groups. Take the time to have deep conversations about their colleagues from diverse cultures as well as the families and children that are part of the program. Is there any cultural group they wish they could know more about? Do they have negative biases toward any of those groups? Many times we are unaware when we are being culturally unresponsive or showing inequities toward others. As a coach, we are not blaming or pointing fingers but asking ourselves and our clients to reflect deeply about whether we are oppressing anyone. Are we promoting inequity in any way in the classroom, the program, or the organization? If so, what steps can we take to make a change? Interestingly, often young children are quite oppressed. Sometimes we make them do things they are simply not interested in doing. We may underestimate their capabilities or have favorites or treat a family differently. Many times all of this happens without us being aware, so bringing awareness to these areas is a crucial first step. Use your coaching sessions to have open conversations in a constructive, relationship-based, strength-focused way to help your client bring consciousness to any other forms of inequity occurring and consider what changes could make things more equitable for everyone.

The next level is to have conversations with your client regarding any biases they have seen reflected in the children and their families or other colleagues in their organization. Talk about these biases and how the client could offer constructive questions to help break them. For example, a preschool teacher had a student who did not want to clean up after finishing his meals. He resisted lifting his own plate. This seemed like defiant or challenging behavior to the teacher. Through questioning and going deeper, the coach and the client developed a plan. The coach asked the client, "What else can you tell me about this child? What do you know about the child's culture? Why do you think the child may not want to clean up the table? What could the child's behavior be communicating to us? How can you find out? Where do you think this behavior may have stemmed from? How could we communicate with the family in a constructive way that we are observing this consistent behavior in the child? How could you deepen your relationship with the child and the family to help support the child's development?" By following these prompts, the teacher was intentional in deepening the relationship with this child. Once this was established, the teacher spoke with the child about why he did not want to clean up after meals. The child answered, "Because women are the ones who are supposed to clean up the table." What a surprise it was for the teacher to hear this! Machismo was part of this child's family culture, and it had become visible in the boy's behavior in the classroom. During conversations with the child and the family, they talked about how biases about gender roles differ in diverse cultures, and the teacher explained that in the classroom culture, everybody cleans up because it helps children develop autonomy. The child shifted his perspective, and he started helping in the classroom after meals.

In this same way, coaching can help your clients see other inequities in the system of early childhood, in their organizations, at the societal level, and on any other level. Through thoughtful questioning, we can help our clients develop a critical eye to identify inequities and lead positive change. By this process, we also work through the barriers that hold down our clients in their own development. Through coaching you can speak with your clients about any roadblocks that were formed by their own culture that are not helping them advance toward equity. For example, a group of family child care providers saw that many things were inequitable for them in their state's Quality Rating and Improvement System (QRIS). They voiced these concerns as a group and organized a meeting with leaders of the state system. However, at the meeting, very few were willing to speak up and share their concerns about inequity in the system. This was because in the culture of many of these providers, they were not accustomed to speaking up or going against the status quo of people in power. They were used to thinking that they did not have the power to change systems at the government level and that they should not mention problems. Even though they had identified problems and had been able to get all the way to a meeting to talk about them, there was still some resistance stemming from those cultural traits that did not allow them to express their concerns. Similarly, through effective questioning you can also help your clients speak up if they feel uncomfortable or have concerns regarding any regulations, assessment tools, scholarships, and so on.

To continue advancing as a society, we must all feel that it is okay to ask questions and bring up concerns in our field, including issues regarding assessment and data. If a client has concerns about any inequities or areas where their needs are not met, then have that conversation with them. Help your client find ways to voice concerns through the appropriate channels and help them feel that they are powerful in everything concerning their work as professionals in early childhood education. It is together that we advance our field to be more uplifting and equitable for all the children and families we serve. But being quiet, compliant, and scared to speak up about our concerns will not get us there. We must voice solutions in an intelligent and constructive way if we are to achieve a better world.

Working in groups with other professionals from the field of early childhood and less as an individual will also help us reach these gains. One person's voice can be very powerful, but groups of voices together can be even mightier. Support your clients in finding groups or other individuals who share the same concerns and passion for change in specific areas of inequity. Encourage your clients to be active participants or even leaders in such initiatives.

Some of us must learn how to have our voices heard. People who are from nondominant cultures may feel repressed or fear to share their voices or perspectives. Whenever a client voices a need or concern, ask questions to help them find ways to express that concern in a constructive and positive way. Ask questions such as these:

- What is the real need?

- Why does this need exist?

- How could this need be fulfilled?

- To whom must we voice this need?

- How can we communicate this in such a way that it will be well received?

- Who are the stakeholders, and what avenues must we use to communicate with them?

- Do you feel comfortable expressing these needs to other stakeholders?

- What positive results could stem from communicating this to other stakeholders?

- What positive effect could you have for children and their families if you voice this need or idea?

- How can I help you go through the process of voicing or expressing this need or idea?

And then be there with your client through that entire process. Help them feel supported and empowered to make a change they want to see in the world.

Revisit the questions on page 83. How have your responses changed? How have they stayed the same?

Competencies

- Set up the stage for coaching with the goal of achieving long-term sustainable change.

- Promote equity through coaching.

- Be equitable with clients.

- Support cultural responsiveness through coaching.

- Support clients in reflecting about dominant cultures.

- Support clients in taking an anti-racist approach in their work in the field of early childhood education.

- Help clients become empowered by learning how to make their voices heard.

Practices

- Consistently listen to your client's voice.

- Speak with your client about their perspectives regarding equity.

- Listen carefully to your client's needs.

- Speak with clients about any inequities in their program.

- Speak with clients about racism.

- Support your client in voicing to different stakeholders any cases of inequities and discrimination.

Hear Your Client's Voice

- What kind of change would you like to see in the field of early childhood education? As your coach, how can I support you advancing toward these changes?

- What areas of inequity do you see in your work in early childhood settings? What could be done to bring change in these areas of inequity?

- How can I support you in breaching any inequities to help you achieve your goals as an early childhood professional?

Hear Your Voice

- What areas of inequity in society have affected you the most? What have you done to voice these areas of inequity?

- Are there any social identities that make you feel uncomfortable? If so, how could you get to know more about those social identities?

- Have you explored your own implicit biases as mentioned in chapter 2?

References and Resources

Bialystok, E. 2011. "Reshaping the Mind: The Benefits of Bilingualism." *Canadian Journal of Experimental Psychology/Revue canadienne de psychologie expérimentale* 65 (4): 229–35.

Freire, Paulo. 2000. *Pedagogy of the Oppressed.* New York: Continuum, 95.

CHAPTER 6

Using Data to Tell a Compelling and Meaningful Story

Culturally responsive data makes visible the uniqueness of each person.

Voices from the Field: Juana

It was the end of a very long day in Juana's early childhood program. The preschoolers in her classroom had been particularly active. She thought perhaps it was because there was a full moon or maybe because of the visitor they'd had that day. She hadn't known there would be a visitor to assess her in her classroom until the young woman suddenly walked in with a notebook and pens. The young woman observed her and the children and took notes with a serious look on her face. That made Juana very tense, especially because she didn't know who this person was or why she was there. Juana let the day advance like normal and tried not to let the visit affect her too much. However, it was raining outside and cold, so they weren't able to do their usual outdoor active morning activities, and the children were squirrelly. Still, Juana did the best she could inside. To help the children with their energy level, they danced to some fun Afro-Cuban beats and other ethnic music she had collected over the years. The early childhood program was in an urban and diverse neighborhood, and representing this diversity was key for Juana. In addition to the rain, the moon, and the unexpected visitor, the day was also uncommon because it was the first day of school for two children who had just emigrated from Brazil. They spoke Portuguese and knew very little English. Juana tried her best to help them feel welcome and comfortable. However, you could tell it was a stressful day for her and for many of the children.

Once all the children went home, Juana cleaned her classroom, turned off the lights, and walked through the quiet hallway. She sighed with relief, knowing she would now get some rest. She walked into the main office to sign out. She bumped into her supervisor and was shocked by what her supervisor told her. "Take this piece of paper with your numbers and do something about it," said her supervisor in a very negative tone. "Now I'm going to have to find funds to get you a coach so that these numbers can increase. The last thing this program needs is more expenses!"

Juana glanced at the sheet of paper, which had some random numbers jotted down. What did these numbers mean? Why was her supervisor angry with her? What did she do wrong? Getting a coach as a punishment for some random numbers? Juana did not have a good evening.

Reflective Questions

- What does data mean to you?

- What does assessment mean to you?

- How do data and assessment affect your work as a coach?

- How can data be used in early childhood programs to advance toward a more equitable society?

- Have you ever had negative experiences with data and assessment? How about your clients?

- How could data be used from a strength-based approach to support your clients in reaching their goals as early childhood professionals?

- What data do you think is essential to collect and use?

- How can you use data to affirm and make your clients' voices more visible?

This chapter emphasizes the use of data as an essential step in a culturally responsive coaching cycle. We present strategies to use qualitative and quantitative data to support the client, to understand and tell their story and that of the childhood settings where they work. In addition, you will learn how to look at data from a strength-based approach, with strategies to use data to empower teachers' professional development. We also look at how to use data in an equitable way. The chapter offers strategies for providing feedback using data and for having deep conversations with your clients on using data to continue improving. We also discuss the current pressure that coaches undergo from organizations to see improvement in data and how to balance those expectations while also coaching for transformative long-term change.

What Is Data?

Commonly, we think of data as numbers and analytics. However, data is much bigger than that. Data is information, and we are literally surrounded by it all the time. As a society, we generally collect data that we value and believe worthy of keeping. The same thing applies to assessment tools. They are usually developed so that we can collect data or the information that we find relevant in our field. So what type of information do we want to collect? What are the values we want to support?

Types of data

Some data is quantitative, which is information described through numbers. For example, quantitative data in early childhood settings includes how many years of experience a teacher has or how many children are enrolled in a classroom. Quantitative data also includes more abstract numbers, like a score that represents an indicator or a descriptor from a specific assessment tool. The number requires us to give it significance and does not have any meaning by itself.

The other type of data is qualitative. We don't necessarily use numbers to represent information for this type of data. We might collect qualitative data through words, images, objects, or videos, among other methods. Qualitative data requires context to have meaning and purpose. It could be a survey of early childhood professionals asking for their ideas regarding a professional development training, or it could be interviews of our clients that help us understand potential needs in the field. Qualitative data can be enriching, giving insights that help us better understand our work.

As a coach, you may have access to data that are both quantitative and qualitative. You may have information about your client's years of education, numbers of hours of professional development completed each year, and so on. You may also have more sophisticated quantitative data, such as scores from assessment or measurement tools that have been used in that client's program, potentially looking at factors such as classroom environment, teacher-child interactions, and administrative scales, among others. And you may be able to collect qualitative data related to your clients. For example, you could create surveys to gather information about your client prior to starting a relationship with them, or you could create an initial focus group with several clients to try to understand areas where you should concentrate your work.

The importance of data

Why is data so important in coaching? Since our goal as coaches is to help our clients reach their goals, having information (data) can help us better serve the needs of our clients. By having data, we can support our field of early childhood education and better serve young children and their families.

Data helps make visible what is happening in early childhood programs. If we don't have data or information, it is much harder to know where to start. By analyzing data, we can bring light to areas where we once saw less clearly, such as systemic racism. By analyzing big chunks of data, we can see trends in how programs have been allocating resources and note specific segments that need more attention. By having data about a particular client, we can see areas of strength as well as areas that may be impeding their well-being and performance. Overall, if data is well used, it can be empowering for our clients and for our society as a whole. But we must be intentional about what kind of data we collect, how we collect it, how we interpret it, and how we use it in decision-making moving forward.

Assessment

This brings us to the topic of assessment. At the most basic level, assessment involves the process of collecting, analyzing, and using data to measure change. At a higher level, assessment is a systematic process of using tools (quantitative or qualitative) to measure changes based on criteria relevant to a particular field. When used as a tool within a culturally responsive coaching process, assessment helps coaches, clients, and the broader community gather information that then can be used to increase awareness, support optimal development, and achieve sustainable change. A tall order for a process that is often associated primarily with punitive decisions!

Reflection

What is your understanding of assessment? What were your experiences with assessments as a child? Were they positive? Was it the same or different for your client? Were important decisions made about you or your client based on the result of assessments?

Many assessment tools in the field of early childhood have been developed as a result of child development theories and child development research, as well as in combination with interdisciplinary fields such as medicine, psychology, and others. Culture plays a critical role in the types of questions that we have asked ourselves in research, which in turn influences assessment tools. For example, we could ask, how can we find out if there is systemic racism in early childhood programs? However, if this question has never been asked, there might not be an assessment tool to collect the information, and we might need to develop one. Evaluation tools evolve alongside our societal values. That's why it's very important for us to start turning a more culturally responsive lens to the assessments we use and those we are developing so that they can reflect the cultures we are trying to collect information about.

In addition to being culturally responsive, we must analyze data from a strength-based approach. This means that whatever data we collect, we want to look at the strengths of the person or group being assessed. Assessment is not supposed to punish, shame, or put down. What would be the purpose of doing that? The purpose of assessment is to help us answer key questions and use that data to make meaningful decisions to grow and improve. It's meant to be an empowering experience: to understand, to tell a story, to appreciate how strong we are already, to support goal setting, to develop a plan, and to celebrate as our clients go through the process of growth.

Sometimes the data has high stakes and can affect a person or a group in a substantial way. For example, a person may lose their job if they don't meet a certain criterion as evaluated by a specific assessment. Or perhaps a program will lose funding if it does not meet a specific benchmark. As coaches, we play a critical role in making sure that the assessment tools and data that are being used in high-stakes ways are analyzed and understood from a culturally responsive perspective. You can ask questions to reflect on the cultural appropriateness of a tool. For example, how was this tool validated? With which cultural groups or settings was it validated? How was the data interpreted? Do any of the questions have implicit biases? How will this data help support the success of the program and the culturally diverse population it serves?

So who decides what data will be collected and what assessments will be conducted? Data may be collected at many different levels. At a macro or population level, data can be collected by the federal, state, county, or city government or by an organization that wants to measure how a segment of the population or programs are performing. Generally the stakeholders in leadership roles at those macro levels decide which data points to collect. At a more micro level, an early childhood program may want to collect data about their centers, a certain age group, or even a particular classroom. Data collection happens at a personal level when you as a coach want to better understand a client.

If data is collected at a macro level for a particular group, for example, to understand the landscape of dual-language learners in early childhood education, stakeholders making decisions on the assessment tool must do it in a way that is culturally and linguistically responsive to the end user, the people being assessed. If not, the assessment may be biased. It is crucial to ask ourselves why we are collecting this data. How will this data affect the end user? Is this data telling a compelling story that will empower the end user? Is this data being collected and analyzed from an equitable standpoint?

These questions are crucial because the data and the assessment tools have financial and societal implications. Data may affect a program's funding or determine how regulations are made at a local, state, and even federal level. Data may affect how resources are dispersed into certain communities. It is important to hear the voices of the stakeholders who will be involved at all steps in collecting and analyzing data, going all the way down to really hearing the voices of families who will be affected by how the data is analyzed and used. It also requires us to think critically so we recognize any inequities occurring because of the way the data is being collected.

Using Data in a Culturally Responsive Way

As a coach in early childhood education, part of your task is likely helping an organization reach its goals. It may require you to work with a client to improve in certain areas that data has shown need growth. Throughout the book we have talked about the importance of individualizing the coaching experience for your client to help them make their own goals. There may be a fine balance between what your client needs and what the organization that has hired you as a coach expects will improve. These two missions do not necessarily need to be disconnected. If we look for areas that are intertwined, we can continue advancing goals for both stakeholders. Being a coach doesn't mean you have to blindly accept all the assessment tools that are used on your clients. You may need to ask deeper-level questions about why specific data is being collected and how it can be used from a strength-based approach for your work with your clients.

Working from a truly culturally responsive coaching perspective starts with your client as the active agent of change. If you want to see long-term change, you need to take a deeper dive in your work individually with each client to speak about their goals, their organization's goals, the children's goals, and the family's goals. What kind of data do we need to understand where we are in progressing toward these goals, and how can we use that information to set long-term goals?

For data to be useful in understanding children, environments, interactions, and even entire programs, it needs to take into account the cultural context in which it is collected, analyzed, and used. But how do we know whether this data reflects the cultural context of our clients? Our favorite answer to this question is "It depends!" For data to be culturally responsive, we need to start by asking ourselves questions that are meaningful to our clients, the context in which we are working, and their aspirations and identified goals. Data is not an end in and of itself; rather, data provides us with information that helps us better understand the person, interaction, or environment. It helps us take meaningful actions and gives us a barometer of progress. It's an essential tool in a systemic and holistic process associated with sustainable change.

No matter the coaching steps you take, data collected through a culturally responsive lens helps you see things you may not have seen before. For example, asking educators about their child-rearing practices and documenting this information can help you understand your client's responses to children. However, more important, the answer makes visible how their beliefs might be affecting that interaction.

Here are some principles that have guided our work in deciding what data to collect and how.

1. **Start with the why.** Beginning with a question related to your client, yourself, or the context in which you work increases the chance the information collected is meaningful. For example, collecting information on how many visits you had with your client may not be meaningful to anyone. It only gives you frequency information, not how responsive you are to your client. However, if you start with the question "Are the number of visits sufficient for my client to make sustainable change?," then the number of visits can be coupled with an analysis of whether you need to increase or decrease the number.

2. **Collect diverse types of quantitative and qualitative data.** Having a variety of information increases the chance of making connections that you may have missed if you collected only quantitative data. And even if you do restrict your data to numbers, considering information from different sources and formats increases the chance that you will have a more complete picture. For example, collecting the number of observations of children that your client makes in and of itself does not guarantee that children will develop to their full potential. But if you add the number of times your client had meetings with the children's families or used the information for planning, those numbers will more likely bring about meaningful change.

3. **Set aside time to reflect throughout the data collection process.** Think of the countless times we've rushed to collect data to submit to a report that was due yesterday. So often it feels like the time invested in collecting the data does not lead to anything significant, other than sleepless nights. When

we do find time to reflect, either by ourselves, with our clients, or at an organization-wide level, it makes a huge difference in how meaningful we feel the data is, how useful it is for making decisions, and whether we have a good return on investment.

In a culturally responsive coaching process, scheduling time to reflect is essential to meet our clients' needs, engage in a meaningful learning process, and optimize the available resources. When we intentionally invest in this reflective practice, our actions become more intentional, we hear diverse voices, and our approach becomes responsive to our clients. By deliberately setting aside time to reflect with our clients, we also mirror the process we hope our clients will undertake. The key is to overcome the challenges to prioritize this essential step and make it routine. The process of analysis and reflection, including strategies, is covered further in this chapter.

Reflection

What principles guide your data collection process? Are the reasons for data collection clear to you, your clients, and the organization at large? Do you have someone to analyze the data and reflect on what it means with you? Two heads are better than one!

Systems for Collecting Data

The scientific method of collecting data encompasses a cyclical process of asking questions, fostering the critical-thinking skills of analyzing, prioritizing, problem solving, and seeing things from different perspectives. It involves gathering information, analyzing and using data, and then coming up with new questions. It is applied in diverse fields and contexts, and it is relevant to a culturally responsive process because it starts by asking questions that are meaningful to the key stakeholders, whether that is our client, the children, the families, or ourselves. The process guides us to identify the questions, collect the information, and hypothesize what the possible action could be. It's not until we test our hypothesis that we know if we got it right. The next round gives us richer information so that eventually our conclusions are the most responsive to our questions.

It is essential to set up a system to collect data that can be used to make decisions and take stock of where we are and how far we have progressed. A culturally responsive data collection system gathers a diversity of meaningful information from many sources, using different approaches to help us get a holistic view of what we are evaluating.

In conversations with colleagues, we have discussed different understandings of the term *system*, which led to diverse interpretations. For example, some colleagues used the term to describe a step-by-step process or way of completing a task. Others understand a *system* as an institution that imposes a way of working that does not reflect reality. To reduce confusion and misinterpretation of what we mean by a culturally responsive data system, we begin by defining how we are using *system* in this context. We use the term *system* to mean that the whole is greater than its parts. In a system, each piece of the puzzle is connected to and influenced by the others. A systems approach connects the dots so that the process is meaningful to the user. Gathering information without knowing the why behind it or linking it to a question leads to meaningless data. Data without analysis and reflection about its meaning just gathers dust, literally or metaphorically.

In a culturally responsive coaching approach, the scientific method guides us to ask four key questions we need to continuously have in our minds to ensure that we are collecting and using meaningful information. Our experience with data has focused on making visible the who, the what, the how, and the reach of the change process. These are the key questions:

1. What meaningful questions do we, our clients, and the organization or early childhood community have that influence our values, beliefs, and practices?

2. What information and what tools do we need to collect to answer these questions?

3. What culturally responsive actions could we take to make positive change happen or lead us back to asking more questions?

4. How well are we doing, and have the goals been achieved for our clients, ourselves, and the supporting organization or community?

To apply these questions in a culturally responsive coaching process, we explore what they mean and provide examples from our experiences working in different settings. As you read through the following paragraphs, reflect on how they align with your values and practices. Have you had similar experiences or seen value in these or similar questions?

What are the meaningful questions, and for whom?

In a culturally responsive approach, we begin the process of asking questions by reflecting on what we want to know in relation to the values, beliefs, and practices that might be influencing a certain behavior or response. For example, our client might ask, "Why does this child keep refusing to use the toilet?" or "Why does this child keep knocking the blocks off the shelf?" By starting from a culturally responsive lens, we could look at our client's beliefs about the appropriate age for children to independently use the toilet and consider whether it is aligned with that of the child's family. Likewise, as coaches, we might ask how our temperament tendencies influence our responses to a client. Do we respond to the child who knocked the blocks off the shelf as being too active, in comparison to our less-active tendency?

It is important to note that a question-asking phase in a system of collecting data can emerge at any point in time. Some questions may come up at the beginning of a client relationship, while others may stem from an event that happens spontaneously or at the end of a planning cycle. Every cycle of questions leads us to a hypothesis, which leads us to ask more questions—but this time we are equipped with more information. This cycle of questions also fosters a reflective approach with our clients and reinforces the idea that we learn through an ongoing process of queries or trials that sometimes we get wrong, which leads to more answers.

What information do we need to collect?

These questions lead us to gather information so we can take culturally responsive actions. But what information do we need? Again, it depends. We can choose almost any type, frequency, and sources. However, the more varied the resources and information, the better equipped we are to come up with meaningful, culturally responsive answers. As is true for good detectives, the more clues we have to make predictions and devise a hypothesis, the better we will be at solving the mystery!

In a culturally responsive approach, where and how this information is collected is critical. Relying on standardized tools to collect information limits our view to what the tools are able to collect. The tools may not be responsive to our inquiries and may not be valid in culturally diverse populations. Gathering information through ongoing observation, interviews, self-reflection exercises, videotaping, surveys, and other qualitative data collection strategies provides a holistic view. For example, a powerful tool we have used to collect information is videotaping our clients as they interact with children throughout their daily routines. The beauty of videos is that they can be stopped, placed in slow motion, and repeated. Videotaping ourselves and our clients also reinforces the disposition to accept our vulnerabilities and trust others not to judge. Other information-gathering strategies in our toolbox come from disciplines outside of education, such as health and agriculture, which we highlight later in this chapter.

SELF-AWARENESS TO ACHIEVE SUSTAINABLE CHANGE

Veena is a family child care educator with over eight years of experience. She has seen scores of children come through her program, including many siblings. She is originally from India, and she often reflects on how she once taught the toddlers the same way she had been taught in school. The teacher asked the questions and gave the information, and the children followed directions. She became aware of how important it was to describe her actions after a training offered by the organization she is partnering with. She started describing what she was doing and what the children were doing. Her older son even noticed, saying, "Mom, it looks like you are talking to yourself." Although Veena realized there was a difference in how she engaged with the children, she still wasn't convinced until she saw the children's responses in the video. By stopping the video at the precise moments, Veena could get the information she needed: children were responding more when she described what they were doing instead of bombarding them with closed-ended questions. She considered how different she and the children felt and how different it was from how she had been taught. Veena has continued to increase her awareness of how she interacts with children and to find ways to be more responsive to each child as she sees new things through the video clips.

What culturally responsive actions will address the questions?

There is a slew of information, resources, advice, and even regulations on what to do or not to do in an early childhood program. Taking action without first going through the two previous steps of asking and collecting meaningful information leads to compliance as opposed to lasting change. Implementing strategies or making changes becomes more culturally responsive, meaningful, and effective if it follows a process of reflection. There is no recipe that fits all situations, and there are no quick fixes when it comes to learning and development. A teacher's actions when a child throws themselves on the floor every time their mother comes to pick them up will depend on the information the teacher has collected about that child. Understanding the child's developmental level, their home environment, and their temperament tendencies will guide the teacher's response. Similarly, when we work with our clients, our actions and theirs are more meaningful and responsive if they are based on our collected information and thoughtful reflection. For example, if a client indicates that they want support with setting up an outdoor space, we gather information about how they plan to use it, what they consider an ideal outdoor environment, what information they already have, and what type of support they need, so they take ownership of the solution. We could easily come in and say, "You need to make it safe, and make sure you have shade and a place to store your equipment." But these easy answers will often lead us to the experience of "entre el dicho y el hecho hay mucho trecho" (In between the saying and the doing is a huge void). The actions we take sometimes lead us back to asking more questions because what we thought would work simply didn't. In the case of the playground, we forgot to ask families what they thought about children playing in the mud!

How well is everyone doing in achieving our goals?

A culturally responsive systems approach focuses on gathering information that captures values, beliefs, and practices from different sources, such as ourselves, our clients, the organization or programs where our clients work, and the broader early childhood community. This, in turn, is used to evaluate progress on our goals and to make meaningful decisions. For example, a client might ask why a child bites so much. A culturally responsive data system uses this question as the starting point to collect information and use it from different perspectives. These different perspectives contribute to identifying and connecting the dots of possible causes, which helps us get a better sense of what action to take. Might the child bite because their teeth are coming in, because they don't have enough language yet to convey their feelings, or because a family member uses a child-rearing practice of biting the child when they bite to show them what it feels like? We take this information we collect to answer questions about how we perceive a particular practice based on our cultural beliefs, couple this information with our client's beliefs, and then juxtapose this with the organization's values. Each piece of the data by itself gets us just so far in understanding why specific interactions such as biting occur. But collectively that information helps us see how each influences the other and guides us to take meaningful action.

A culturally responsive data collection system also builds awareness about how assumptions can be detrimental to children, our clients, and the early childhood community. For example, merely looking at a standardized tool might show a particular family child care with a low score because our client uses their living room and kitchen to carry out activities with the children. Without understanding the context of the environment, the resources available, and our client's and the families' perspectives, that score might indicate that the program is not doing too well, instead of acknowledging that the FCC educator put a sustainable practice and solution in place that protects children's well-being.

HEARING ALL VOICES LEADS TO SUSTAINABLE CHANGE: Reflections from Jill

A local organization wanted to ensure that each child had received at least three observations for each curriculum objective by the time educators had their three-month meeting with the parents. The supervisors were concerned that educators were not completing the required observations, even though it didn't seem like an impossible task, and it was not reflecting well on their organization. I was hired to help educators comply with the required tasks. As I started working with the educators, I asked them to share why they had chosen early childhood and how they saw their role in relation to the children. Most of them answered that they enjoyed working with children and felt that they made a difference in children's lives. I then asked them what was the most challenging part of their work, and the majority responded that it was completing the paperwork for the child assessment system. When I asked them why, they answered that they were not savvy with technology or felt that it took them away from being present with the children. These two data sources helped me understand the bigger picture and how they influenced each other. When I asked the educators what would help them complete this requirement, they emphasized needing more practice with technology and better ways to optimize their time so that they didn't lose time away from the children. Over the next couple of months, I set up small-group sessions after hours to practice using the online system, which helped alleviate the stress associated with technology. However, it wasn't until the educators started looking at the pictures that they routinely took of the children to document their learning that the educators got excited about assessment. They realized they had never connected their usual documentation routine to the online system because they completed this step on a quarterly basis. Once educators started getting into the habit of uploading their pictures and using the information to understand the children, the number of required observations they completed increased.

Making Data Meaningful

When we couple meaningful data to values, beliefs, and practices from different perspectives, sustainable change happens. But we must also ask, "Meaningful to whom?" To help answer this question, we have used two complementary types of information-gathering processes that we feel are essential to a culturally responsive coaching process, qualitative and quantitative. Because we present quantitative data in numerical form, it tends to be perceived as more objective, while qualitative data is more subjective. However, from our experiences, this is often not the case. When quantitative data is measured using culturally biased tools, it produces culturally biased results, which in turn leads to harmful decisions that impact our clients and the children and families with whom they work. In contrast, qualitative data that truly captures the key stakeholder's voice can be a powerful tool that describes the essence of what is going on and can describe what numbers can't.

Reflection

Have you taken the time to reflect on the culture that the tool is based on and how it aligns with your client's culture? Have you found yourself in a situation in which the data you received do not coincide with your cultural beliefs?

Experts from diverse fields, including the sciences, marketing, and community health, all tackle the problem of making data meaningful for different stakeholders, just as we do in the early childhood field. For example, scientists gather data on how diverse individuals walk on varied terrain to see how to build prosthetic devices that are accessible in terms of type of gait, expense, and ease of use. Community health workers gather data on human behavior and beliefs to identify how vaccinations can reach people in urban and rural areas effectively. Marketing companies gather data about diverse populations to identify what they need and determine how to reach them in meaningful and effective ways. Each of these groups is trying to figure out what questions are meaningful and to whom, how to collect useful and effective information to help answer meaningful questions, and how to reflect and analyze this information with key stakeholders to spur action. This section presents a sample of data collection processes that originated outside of the education field but have been used, contributed toward, or achieved positive outcomes in early childhood.

The first comprehensive system is positive deviance (PD), and the other is Participatory Learning and Action (PLA). The first started in the discipline of nutrition to combat malnutrition, and the latter as an agricultural extension tool to improve farming practices. The processes of listening to the stakeholders' voices to ask meaningful questions and together come up with sustainable solutions transfers easily to other disciplines.

Positive deviance is a process of identifying behaviors that helped solve a problem even as others had negative results. In the face of all types of problems, there are people (or situations), the positive deviances, who have found a way of succeeding with the resources they have while others in the same environment still struggle or haven't figured out how to use their resources. Through a positive deviance approach, expertise and solutions are found in the people most affected by the situation. The outside entities must have the mindset that they are not the experts—the stakeholders in the trenches living and experiencing the challenges are the real experts, with true understanding of what is going on and how it can be solved. Coming in from the outside with questions, data, and solutions that may have worked elsewhere does not foster ownership, respect, nor sustainable change. It is through listening to the key stakeholders' stories that the group formulates questions to identify the positive deviances. Listening to their voices leads to reflection and ultimately applying local solutions that achieve meaningful impact.

What does positive deviance look like in a culturally responsive coaching process? Our answer again is that it depends. How open are we to looking for the positive deviances in data? Do we aggregate the information so much that it loses the details of the origins of that information? We need different levels of detail to make executive decisions at various levels of program implementation. For example, information on specific children is essential to draw conclusions at a classroom or FCC level. But at a program level, aggregating the information to get the averages or ranges helps a director get a sense of how the program is doing overall.

A director who takes the time to search for abnormalities, not to catch someone's mistake but to understand what that data means, will more likely identify positive deviances. When we analyze data, we usually find what we are looking for or what we expect to see. The trick is to look at data unfiltered so that we can see things we never saw before. Discovering that the children in a particular classroom have reached higher levels of development than their same-age peers in other classrooms is an opportunity to ask follow-up questions: Is something happening in this group of children that is worth learning about? What could be beneficial to others in my program?

As a coach, you might find yourself looking at data across your clients and seeing that one of your clients asks a great deal of open-ended questions and children are engaged in conversation with each other. This could open up a conversation with your client about what is prompting the conversations and where or how this skill was learned. When you understand what contributes to your client's behavior that deviates in a positive direction (asking open-ended questions and fostering conversations) you can use the information to help your other clients in changing their behavior, since they share similar realities.

Participatory Learning and Action is an approach used to monitor, evaluate, and learn from program implementation. It began in 1980 as a tool to assess the impact of agricultural initiatives, emphasizing that assessment without action does not lead to sustainable change. This approach's philosophical principles underscore how important it is that the evaluation gives the power of knowledge to those most affected by the initiative, program, or actions. A common phrase in this approach is "handing over the baton to the participants." By reversing the power of decision to the community, educator, or even the child, meaningful information emerges and sustainable change is possible.

One PLA tool is pairwise ranking. It prioritizes a list of multiple options or challenges by rating each option against the others and then ranking them by which one is selected the most often. The process leads to a numerical rating of what is most to least important. Although it may be confusing the first time you use it, once you follow the steps and see how practical it is, you will find multiple applications in your professional and personal life. For example, a group of early childhood teachers and their supervisors were asked to identify the five top factors that influenced their daily interactions with children. They selected the PLA pairwise ranking tool to help them determine which factor had the highest impact and which factor they could best control. They drew a table and placed each factor in the right-hand column and repeated the same list in the same order on the top row. Then they compared each factor against the other and selected the one that had the most impact on their work with the children. How they defined *impact* was left to them to decide. They started by first comparing *planning time* with *well-being*. They selected planning time as more important because if they had the time to plan, their well-being would be positively affected. They then continued to compare *planning time* with *available materials* and selected planning time again. They continued down the row, selecting which factor was more important based on their reasoning. In some cases, both factors were equally important, as when they compared *well-being* with *working with families*. They felt that their own well-being influenced working with families and working with families affected the children. They then counted how many times one factor was selected over the other, coming up with a list that ranked them from highest to lowest score. The table on page 113 is the completed pairwise ranking grid. A similar process can be implemented with educators and families around key indicators of quality, or even be used on a personal level to make career and life-balance choices. It's an example of how qualitative and quantitative data can complement each other.

	Planning time	Well-being	Available materials	Working with families	Support from supervisor
Planning time		Planning time	Planning time	Working with families	Support from supervisor
Well-being			Well-being	Well-being & Working with families	Support from supervisor
Available materials				Working with families	Support from supervisor
Working with families					Support from supervisor
Support from supervisor					
Total times selected	2	2	0	3	4

HANDING OVER THE OWNERSHIP OF DATA GATHERING

As part of a family engagement event, a local organization invited two speakers to present to families about accessing community services in Washington, DC. The first speaker was from a local organization that offered a variety of health, education, legal, and job placement services. They were heavily involved in the community and were known for the quality of their clients' services, but recently enrollment numbers in their education and health programs had been declining. The other speaker was from a partner organization supporting local early childhood programs. The first speaker shared information through PowerPoints and colorful leaflets, while the families sat in chairs and listened to the presentation. The second speaker began by laying out chart paper and dozens of markers on the floor. The families were asked to stand up and make a circle around the chart paper. The speaker drew the first line on the paper, saying, "This is Fourteenth Street as it crosses through this neighborhood." The families nodded. The speaker asked the families what services they found important that were located along Fourteenth Street or its crossroads. The first person who spoke was handed a marker, aka "the baton." They were asked to locate the service on the paper with a symbol. Little by little, as families mentioned another service, they were "handed the baton" in turn. Soon everyone was engaged in populating their community map. When families had completed their mapping, they were asked which services were missing that they would like to see on the map. Again, the families began to identify these services and locate them on the map in places convenient for them. Interestingly, services that the first presenter mentioned were not drawn on the map at first, even though they already existed. It goes to show that information giving is not the same as taking ownership of the information. It doesn't matter how many times we give out information; the data-collection process is more powerful when the user takes ownership.

So, how can PLA be applied in a culturally responsive coaching process? As before, it depends! How open are you to trying new ways of listening and increasing your clients' power to make decisions? How open are you to putting your agenda on hold to go with your clients'? Just as infants and toddlers know best how to explore the world, what a gift we can give our clients when they can take the baton and identify the information that is important to them.

Revisit the questions on page 96. How have your responses changed? How have they stayed the same?

Practices

- Foster critical-thinking skills: analyze, prioritize, problem solve, see things from different perspectives.

- Expand the use of diverse quantitative and qualitative data-collection strategies that look at the whole person or program.

- Advocate for a system of data collection that is culturally responsive and offers meaningful information for you, your client, and the broader early childhood community.

- Put your own beliefs and values on hold to clear your filters so that you can see things you may not have seen before.

- Embrace the scientific method of starting with a question, collecting information to form a hypothesis of why something might be happening, and continuing the iterative cycle of using the data to test, create new questions, and collect information.

Hear Your Client's Voice

- How will your client's voice, including their beliefs, values, and practices, be enhanced through a culturally responsive data system?

- How can you use data to make your clients visible?

- What are some of the challenges you might encounter as you expand and strengthen your data collection systems to be culturally responsive to your clients?

Hear Your Voice

- How has the information presented in this chapter changed or affirmed your practice of collecting and using data?

- What specific strategies do you find useful to build on your strength of being a culturally responsive coach?

- How can you use the information in this chapter to advocate that others celebrate how data can make visible the uniqueness of your clients?

Hear Other Stakeholders

- How can the broader early childhood community benefit from a culturally responsive data system?

- Have you found organizations or other examples outside of the early childhood community that are implementing culturally responsive data systems?

References and Resources

Center on the Developing Child, Harvard University. n.d. "Frontiers of Innovation." https://developingchild.harvard.edu/innovation-application/frontiers-of-innovation.

Cowles, Henry. 2017. "Child's Play: The Authoritative Statement of Scientific Method Derives from a Surprising Place—Early 20th-Century Child Psychology." https://aeon.co/essays/how-the-scientific-method-came-from-watching-children-play.

Foundation for Child Development. www.fcd-us.org.

Kenton, Nicole. n.d. "Participatory Learning and Action (PLA)." www.iied.org /participatory-learning-action-pla.

Positive Deviance Collaborative. https://positivedeviance.org.

Russell, Tim. n.d. "Pair Wise Ranking Made Easy." https://pubs.iied.org/sites/default /files/pdfs/migrate/G01675.pdf.

CHAPTER 7

Building Resilience through a Culturally Responsive Approach

It takes a trusting, understanding, and empathetic village to build resiliency.

—A family child care educator from Liberia

Voices from the Field: Maria and Reyna

A listener, empathetic, humble, incredibly intelligent, a mother and a wife with her own struggles who overcame a great deal: that was Maria. A coach, early childhood specialist, trainer, friend, mother, and amazing woman. She is no longer with us, but she left the indelible legacy of her passion for valuing and inspiring early childhood educators. Reyna is an example of the lasting effect she had on others. Reyna is a loving, compassionate family child care owner who immigrated to this country as a young woman. Many years ago, thanks to Maria's mentorship and passion for early childhood, Reyna opened up her own family child care business to make sure her sons had a strong beginning while remaining in a familiar environment. Reyna never forgot Maria's kind words and encouragement. They continue to accompany her today and have benefited the many children who have come through her program. Now, fifteen years later, her grown sons are her tech and moral support. They helped her learn to videotape her interactions and share them with her coach so that she can fine-tune her ability to see children through their eyes, carefully observing the details in their movements and what they are saying.

In 2020 everyone in Reyna's family contracted COVID-19, and she had to close her family child care business for a few weeks. Suddenly, having to take care of herself gave her a new perspective on life. She often says, "It's the people who have supported you along the way that make you stronger. It's the people who mirror the importance of a trusting relationship that make the journey so much richer." She has gone through enormous transitions and has had to adapt to the new reality while constantly supporting her own family. Yet she feels she will get through this too. Having had a trusting mentor years ago and connecting with other early childhood professionals have contributed to her resiliency and the support of those who are now a part of her village.

Reflective Questions

- Have you had someone in your life help you to get over challenges? Do you know whether your clients have or have had someone to lean on?

- What is your definition of resilience?

- What has influenced your resiliency?

- Have you encountered moments when you have felt overwhelmed and stressed? How did your body respond to this stress? Could you listen to what your body was telling you? Do you feel a change in your muscles when you de-stress?

- What do you do when you are stressed? Do you have someone to support you? How does it affect your thought process and interactions with others?

- How does your culture perceive stress, challenges, or failure?

- Do you work with educators who have had adverse experiences in their lives? Do you know if and how they overcame them?

- Do you feel you are resilient? Do you know what your individual needs are to become resilient? Do you know what each of your clients' needs are?

- What strengths do you and each of your clients have that build resilience?

Cultural responsiveness is an essential protective factor for building resilience. When we engage in a dialogue with our clients about who they are and their challenges and successes, we connect as human beings. As we interact with our clients, we also become aware of our own cultural filters that have influenced who we are and how we overcame obstacles. This self-awareness is meant to create empathy, as no one is free from encountering adversity and stress in some way or another.

This chapter explores what is meant by resilience and how a culturally responsive coaching process can counterbalance moments of stress and uncertainty and help our clients become stronger. We explore how beliefs, values, and practices influence how we confront challenges. We also present different strategies that support our clients and ourselves in becoming more resilient. Although we wrote this book during the COVID-19 pandemic, which required confronting and adapting to new ways of life across the globe, the conversation about resilience and factors contributing to overcoming stress is timeless.

This chapter continues the conversation about how our clients' interactions influence their professional journey and their programs' quality. The relationship that we build with our clients through these ongoing conversations includes mirroring a process of self-awareness and building an understanding of what triggers our stress. Throughout this chapter, we highlight the importance of a culturally responsive approach to address adverse experiences that contribute to stress, and we share practices that build foundational skills to overcome them. This chapter also helps us strengthen the foundations of trusting relationships and foster our clients' resilience by listening to their voices.

How does stress affect our coping mechanisms?

Brain research confirms what we instinctively have known for many years. When we foster trusting relationships as a foundation of all interactions, children build a positive sense of self as well as problem-solving skills, self-compassion, and the agency to confront adversity. Thus, children's overall well-being and learning are enhanced through these interactions. Likewise, as adults, our relationship building continues to be vital, especially as a counterbalance to the ongoing challenges we face.

We may have felt stressed before a test or before starting a new job. Stress is part of being human. Sometimes stress can even be beneficial. It's our body's natural way of keeping us alert and engaged in the task. In our reflections with our clients, we often see that their stress comes from wanting to excel, whether it is mastering a new technology or following new regulations. Their bodies relax, and it seems like a heavy weight has been lifted when they recognize that their stress is a natural response to stepping out of their comfort zones. Stress is normal, and at the right levels, it can even propel us forward.

Reflection

Can you think of times when you felt stressed because of a test, new job, or moving to a new place? How did stress affect you? Do you know how your clients respond to these transitions? How do your clients react to stress? What experiences have caused stress in their lives?

However, when stress levels increase or stress is constant, our thinking and sense of control can get derailed. When our hearts beat quickly nonstop and the adrenaline is on overdrive, levels of cortisol, a stress hormone in our bodies, increases. This causes the part of the brain responsible for reasoning and problem solving to slow down. When extreme stress levels don't subside over time, they have lifelong repercussions on our learning and overall well-being. Suppose you have worked with children and families who have constantly struggled to meet monthly payments, have experienced extreme violence in their neighborhoods or even at home, or have dealt with alcoholism and drug abuse. In that case, you can witness the detrimental effect this toxic stress has on the mind and body. We know that children who grow up in these environments are more likely to have school problems, learning delays, limited self-control, and undeveloped problem-solving skills.

Reflection

Have you had similar experiences with how adversity affects overall well-being, either personally or through others? What types of adversity did you or people you know have to face in their early years? How did it affect you, or the people you know, in your adult life? How has that influenced your perception of adversity?

What is resilience, and how does it counterbalance adversity and stress?

Our understanding of what resilience is and how it is achieved varies according to whom we talk to. In our conversations with clients, sometimes resilience is perceived as something we have or don't have. It's seen as an inner strength that allows us to withstand moments of crisis. For others, resilience is associated with skills that are learned. These skills lead us to persevere and overcome stress or adversity.

Within the context of a culturally responsive coaching framework, we think of resilience as something we can achieve thanks to three overarching actions:

1. Building a positive, trusting relationship, which provides the security to take risks and move out of our comfort zones.

2. Establishing a safe and responsive environment, which helps build confidence in ourselves and others.

3. Developing critical higher-order thinking skills, which leads to acquiring self-control, problem-solving skills, and flexibility.

These skills are the foundation for more than just getting through bad situations. They are essential for overall well-being and learning. Without these critical components, we cannot overcome adversity, nor can we achieve our fullest potential.

When we think back to moments of adversity in our lives, we may find that we overcame them with the support of people we trusted who believed in us. We may find that an ability to look at problems as opportunities helped us figure out how to resolve the issue we faced. Perhaps looking at the situation from different angles opened new possibilities.

BUILDING RESILIENCE AND SOLACE:
A Composite Reflection from Childhood

It happened again. My parents were shouting at each other for no apparent reason, oblivious to everyone in the room. This time it was my brother knocking over a cup of milk during dinner that triggered it. My father suddenly sprang to his feet to avoid a river of milk in his lap. His brusque movements startled all of us and unleashed the yelling. The day had been especially stressful for him. He'd had an interview for a job that he was overqualified for, but it was the only one that did not require him to speak English.

Back home, he had been a successful business owner, and our lives seemed so simple then. We lived near my grandmother, aunt, uncles, and a slew of cousins. We freely played in the park until our parents called us in at dusk. Lunchtime was my favorite time of the day. We sat around the table sharing what happened at school in the morning and excitedly talked about our plans with our cousins and friends later in the afternoon. Of course, no play was allowed until after we completed our homework.

In the United States, everything seemed different. Our family meals were in the evenings, and everyone seemed too tired or stressed to engage in any conversation or feel patience when we spilled milk. Our mom cooked from boxes and cans, lacking time to prepare food with fresh products bought from the local market. Her professional life changed too. She had to learn to drive and use the computer to be competitive in the job market. My siblings and I also had to adjust. My mom dropped me off early in the morning at Mama Pierce's family child care, and I was the last one to get picked up late in the day.

Mama Pierce was always at the door to greet me with a smile and a warm hug. I played with my friends, sang songs, and savored her home cooking. It was almost like being back in my country.

I also remember taking solace in my room to get away from my parents' fighting. Sometimes I watched the dust sparkles caught in sunlight dancing across my bedroom, which always dissipated my sorrow. My older sister sometimes would join me. I was so lucky to have an older sister who knew the precise moment and technique to puff up the usually mundane dust specks into the air to catch the setting sun rays. As we gazed into this natural wonder, we got lost in its simple, accessible beauty.

Reflection

Have you had similar experiences in your childhood? Have your clients? How have you overcome adverse situations? What experiences of resiliency do you have? How have your clients overcome adverse situations? Do you or your clients see resilience as something that you are born with, something that develops due to interactions with the environment, or some mix of the two?

A positive, trusting relationship greatly influences resilience. These relationships affect our sense of self. The interactions that foster problem solving, creativity, and agency in a person lead to resilience. Interactions that prioritize compliance and following regulations without understanding the why behind these regulations and how they can be beneficial lead to stagnation. Stagnation does not build resilience; it creates a sense of mistrust in oneself and others.

MASTERING TECHNOLOGY WITH EMPATHETIC SUPPORT

After she retired, Paulette launched a new career as an early childhood educator. She had raised her children and was very much involved in caring for children in the neighborhood and the church she regularly attended. However, she had never used a computer before. The first day she received a laptop from a sponsoring organization, she looked at it and felt immobilized, not knowing where to start. It was a completely foreign object that lay on her lap. Through her coach's ongoing support, along with trusting in her own competence and building on her strengths amid her colleagues' cheering, her computer skills slowly emerged. Her resilience grew not because she needed to comply with the licensing agency by submitting reports and uploading observations, but because she realized she had the competence and inner drive to make it happen.

Reflection

How do you support your clients in balancing the need to comply with regulations while building competencies associated with resiliency? How do you integrate licensing standards into your coaching role so that your clients feel supported and understood?

As coaches, we need to continue fostering resilience and problem-solving skills in ourselves and our clients. This is especially true when we are faced with challenging situations. The way we face difficult moments, whether personal, professional, or economic, influences our stress level—and overall well-being—in our interactions with others and ultimately the children we serve.

Times of great uncertainty, stress, and needing to adapt to an ever-changing world are a constant in our lives. Some people find ways to get through crises better than others. Culturally responsive coaching has building trusting relationships at its core. This includes intentionally listening to understand rather than respond by giving our client time to talk without interrupting or judging or looking for a particular phrase that we want to hear. This form of listening sends the message to our clients that what they have to say is important, and they feel heard. Through responsive interactions, we prepare ourselves and our clients to confront stress, helping them become resilient problem solvers who are adaptable to ongoing change.

The Effect of Temperament, Cultural Values, Beliefs, and Practices on Stress

Adversity affects people in different ways. And how each person responds to challenges is also distinct. Our temperament tendencies and how we respond to our environment, people, and situations influence our reactions to new or unexpected events. If you are born with a high sensitivity to touch and loud noises, the sound of a door slamming can make you jump, but that same sound may not affect someone who has a lower sensitivity. Someone with a flexible temperament tendency may perceive adversity that requires change as an opportunity, but for others who naturally require time to adjust, this can be stressful or even paralyzing.

Although we come into this world with some established temperament tendencies, our responses evolve based on the interaction between our genetic makeup and the surrounding environment. Likewise, our self-esteem and early messaging we received about our competencies influence how we respond to change. When we feel competent and understand that making mistakes is a way of learning, we can better problem solve and overcome challenges.

Our cultural values, beliefs, and practices influence the level of stress we have and how we handle stress in our lives. For example, how we accomplish tasks and respond to stress depends on our perception of time, which is influenced by our cultural beliefs. Do you see time as linear, with a defined beginning and end, with the emphasis placed on deadlines and accomplishing tasks? Or do you see time as an iterative process, with tasks moving through a cyclical process of starting, moving, and starting over again, so the journey is more important than the finish line? Some people respond to deadlines and clearly defined steps that need to be accomplished, while others thrive when the timeline is fluid and they are encouraged to learn from their mistakes.

The change process is full of uncertainty and may lead to moments of angst for our clients and ourselves. No matter how carefully we establish the cycle of coaching, we are bound to come to moments when the best laid plans fall through, especially in times of crisis. Perhaps the goals set were not the right ones, the tasks that were spelled out in the coaching plan did not achieve the results we were expecting, or something happened with a child or family that means we have to entirely shift gears.

What can we do as coaches to build our clients' resilience? How can we become aware of our clients' situations to support their overall well-being? How can we use this information to increase trusting relationships that will form the basis of their professional learning and resilience? How can the essential skills of listening, showing empathy, and practicing self-compassion be incorporated into our work with clients to counterbalance their adverse experiences and those of the families they serve? This next section offers a range of practices we have found to support our clients' resilience and give them the tools to do the same with the children and families in their care. They are key practices that we have relied on in our interactions that build clients' capacity to cope, heal, and become their own change agents. Some of these practices, such as building a trusting relationship, we have discussed in other chapters through different lenses. These practices' repetitive nature emphasizes how interconnected the various stages, the strategies of your coaching relationship, and the progress to sustainable change really are.

Culturally Responsive Practices to Confront Challenges and Build Resilience

A culturally responsive approach is a fundamental element to building resilience in times of change and in times of stress. We need to ask ourselves as coaches how our interactions and our responsiveness with our clients can help counterbalance adverse situations. Our responsive approach is based on the following overarching principles:

1. Building positive, trusting relationships to provide the security to take risks and move out of our comfort zone

2. Establishing a safe and responsive environment to build confidence in ourselves and others

3. Developing critical higher-order thinking skills to acquire self-control, problem-solving skills, and flexibility

We put these principles into practice through the strategies listed here. As you read these practices, reflect on the ones that resonate with you and which ones are new. Have you found that some have worked better than others when you or your clients have faced adversity? Which have contributed to your resilience and that of your clients?

Trust yourself and be open to being vulnerable

One voice that we need to hear sometimes with more appreciation is our own. Sometimes we act like we are our worst enemy and second-guess ourselves. The negative voices that run through our minds, especially when under stress, sometimes interfere with our inner voice of compassion, understanding, and vulnerability. When we learn to trust ourselves and practice self-compassion, we can be strong enough to admit and share our vulnerabilities. Stating "I don't know" or "I too feel afraid" shows that we trust ourselves enough to share with our clients. It demonstrates practices that they can use with children and families in turn and also contributes to fostering a trusting relationship.

QUIETING THE VOICES OF SELF-DOUBT:
Reflections from Jill

Carolyn has coached me for a few years now. The coaching relationship began by her asking me what drove me to get up in the morning. My answer was, "Knowing that I'm making a difference in the lives of children and their families." Over the next four years, I felt an ebb and flow of trust in myself, wondering whether I was still fulfilling this drive. Thanks to the ongoing dialogue, acceptance, and understanding from Carolyn, my trust in myself has grown immensely. This trust is distinct from self-esteem. I have a positive image of myself and know I am competent. Having trust in myself manifests in my sense of agency and ability to foster sustainable change, as opposed to compliance. Whenever I feel this trust wane, I practice a technique that we talked about frequently. First, I acknowledge that those voices of distrust exist. Next, I give the positive and negative voices a name and then have them talk to each other without judgment, using empathy to minimize the power of self-doubt. I named the voices that believe in my ability to make a difference in the lives of children "Victoria." The voice that distrusts my capacity to make a difference I called "Mana." At first, I would try to ignore Mana, but then Carolyn encouraged me to have a conversation of understanding with both voices, to let them know that it's normal to feel uncertain or discouraged. I now engage Victoria in discussion with Mana so that Victoria's positive energy gently yet firmly quiets Mana's voice. Moments of uncertainty continue to emerge, but I am armed with tools to get past them.

Reflection

Have you ever doubted or mistrusted yourself? How did that make you feel? Were you able to share your feelings with others? What strategies do you have that build trust in yourself and your ability to fulfill your mission? Do you know if your clients have had similar feelings? Have they been able to share them with you? How do they get past those moments?

Build trust by listening to understand, not to respond

How you perceive your client influences your interactions. When you trust their knowledge, competency, agency, and intentions, your interactions come from a strength-based approach. As coaches, when we search for our clients' strengths, we make them more visible—sometimes bringing out strengths that our clients did not even know they had! As we show our sense of trust in their competency and intentions and how we value their role, our clients' resilience grows.

Trusting others involves putting aside our judgments of the other person's responses long enough to understand them. It requires going into the relationship with an open mind, confident that trust begets trust. When clients feel they are really heard and accepted for who they are, they are more likely to be open about the challenges they are facing. Trust builds self-confidence and can help them move out of their comfort zones. Knowing that someone takes the time to really hear them and has their back strengthens resilience.

As described throughout this book, trusting relationships are built when we put aside our agenda and lean into what our clients are saying, doing, or feeling. We build trusting relationships with clients similarly to how we build trusting relationships with children—engaging in responsive dialogue that emphasizes listening to their voices by allowing enough time for our clients to tell their stories and trusting that what they have to say is important and valid. We avoid asking leading questions or questions that have a right or wrong answer. During challenging times, what a gift to our clients to have a listening ear that does not judge them! They can then focus on getting past challenging times because they have someone who believes in their competency.

Foster self-care and compassion in yourself and your clients

As members of a caring profession, our mission is to show compassion for others and support their overall well-being. However, we often invest so much time looking out for others that we forget to look out for ourselves. When faced with adversity or crisis, our bodies take on the burden of keeping us going. This additional burden slowly eats away at our bodies' reserves, and it can ultimately lead to a point where our bodies say, "Enough!"

Likewise, our commitment to excellence may push us not to accept mistakes, either from our clients or from ourselves. The cultural beliefs we grew up with might have frowned upon making mistakes or perceived them as a weakness.

Being compassionate to ourselves and our clients, especially during moments of adversity, helps overcome any message of weakness.

One strategy that we have increasingly relied on throughout our profession is the practice of mindfulness. Focusing on the here and now, zeroing in on the sounds and sensations around us, redirects our minds to things we have control over. It sounds so simple to sit in your living room, in a car, or on a park bench and tune out your thoughts by focusing on the sounds around you. But it is amazing how much rest your mind gets from not having to work so hard thinking of everything at the same time. Practicing mindfulness gives us a break from the constant demands of planning, acting, and showing results. Many mindfulness exercises and apps are available to guide you, and we have included some links at the end of this chapter to help you make mindfulness a part of your daily practice.

Foster flexibility and innovation through problem solving

Adversity or crisis situations can discombobulate our routines and daily practices. Looking at the situation from different perspectives and possibilities and focusing on innovation and problem solving can help resolve the issues and build our resilience. As with other aspects of personality and temperament, innovation and problem-solving competencies are influenced by our cultural beliefs. If a culture is focused on compliance, then finding new ways to address issues through problem solving and innovation may not be encouraged. Compliance could instead stifle these critical skills. When we ask our clients open-ended questions and infuse strategies such as situational analysis, brainstorming, and prioritization to reflect on the underlying causes and solutions for a situation, no matter how unlikely they sound, we support our clients in becoming more resilient. For example, we can work through a strengths, weaknesses, opportunities, and threats (SWOT) situational analysis process to identify the strengths and weaknesses that pertain to a situation and then identify the external opportunities or threats. When we brainstorm, we come up with ideas without judging any of them as right or wrong. This brain dumping liberates us to come up with novel ideas. Prioritization helps us to feel like we can start moving forward, especially when faced with so many possibilities. There are many more tools, ranging from the simple to the complex, that can help you and your clients take stock of what is happening and get a grasp of the situation from different angles.

Reframe a worrying mindset into a learning mindset

It is normal to feel worried about the future or to focus on the negative when faced with adversity or challenges. This tendency to worry can be exacerbated by cultural beliefs and practices that emphasize dependency. Acknowledging that these feelings exist is the first step in taking control over them so that you can redirect the energy and focus on the excitement that comes from learning, including making mistakes.

LEARNING DURING A PANDEMIC

When the COVID-19 pandemic hit the United States in March 2020, many early childhood programs had to close their doors and switch to online interactions and learning. Amima, an early childhood educator working with toddlers, felt that her world had turned upside down. How was she going to engage with toddlers through this new medium? How would she learn how to use all of this fancy technology, when she already found using the computer to write up her observations a challenge? Thanks to her supervisor's patience and support, she was able to turn it into an opportunity. Her supervisor met with other coordinators to form a plan. Since they worked closely with families, they found an opportunity to strengthen that connection and bring parents into the process of planning. Amima asked the parents of the infants what materials they had at home, such as empty boxes and food cartons, nonbreakable bottles, and scarves. She then asked parents to come up with how they could play with their child using those materials instead of the teachers dictating what to do. Parents came up with great ideas, such as punching holes in a food carton, painting wheels on the side, and having their child pull it around the house. Amima and her colleagues became excited about using parents' ideas and making videos to share with families, showing how they could engage with their infants by using materials at hand. Although this pandemic has led to a great deal of uncertainty and angst, the support from supervisors, coaches, and colleagues has turned it into a learning opportunity for all.

Stay connected to your inner self and others

In times of uncertainty and strife, reconnecting to who we are as individuals and members of a community provides us the needed support to counterbalance these adverse experiences. Taking time to reflect on what drives us and where we get our energy keeps us grounded in what is truly important to us. Whether we get the energy from within or from others, reconnecting to what is essential helps to replenish what we lose when facing adversity or crisis. When we connect to our values and our sense of who we are, our actions are guided by this foundation. Similarly, when we guide our clients to reconnect to their values and identify where they get their energy, they replenish their toolbox of coping strategies. Asking simple questions can help our clients, and ourselves, take action: "How much energy does this (action, idea, interaction) give you?" "Which value does this (action, idea, interaction) connect to?" "Does what you are doing or feeling align with how you want to demonstrate your values?"

Revisit the questions on page 118. How have your responses changed? How have they stayed the same?

Competencies

- Trust yourself.

- Trust others.

- Build a trusting relationship to build resilience.

- Foster self-care and compassion in yourself and your clients.

- Foster innovation and problem solving.

- Be flexible.

- Reduce stress.

- Build empathy.

- Reframe your mindset when facing stress to one of learning, not just worrying.

- Stay connected to who you are and to others.

Hear Your Client's Voice

- What will you continue to do or start doing to foster your client's resilience?

- How can you better understand your client's story of their cultural beliefs related to resilience and change?

Hear Your Voice

- What will you do to build your circle of support?

- How will you use the information in this chapter to strengthen your resiliency?

References and Resources

Center on the Developing Child, Harvard University. n.d. "Resilience." https:// developingchild.harvard.edu/science/key-concepts/resilience.

Elsey, Emma-Louise. 2015. "Every Coach Should Use This Easy Tool to Boost Their Business: SWOT Analysis." International Coaching Federation (ICF). https:// coachingfederation.org/blog/every-coach-should-use-this-easy-tool-to-boost -their-business-swot-analysis.

———. 2015. "Feeling Stuck? You'll Love These 5 Easy to Remember Brainstorming Questions." International Coaching Federation (ICF). https://coachingfederation .org/blog/feeling-stuck-youll-love-5-easy-remember-brainstorming-questions.

———. 2015. "Urgent-Important Matrix: A Time Management Tool for Coaches and Clients." International Coaching Federation (ICF). https://coachingfederation.org /blog/urgent-important-matrix-a-time-management-tool-for-coaches-and-clients.

Hackbert, Lucianne, and Maria Gehl. n.d. "Getting Started with Mindfulness: A Toolkit for Early Childhood Organizations." www.zerotothree.org/resources/2896-getting -started-with-mindfulness-a-toolkit-for-early-childhood-organizations.

The Institute of Coaching, McLean, Affiliate of Harvard Medical School. 2020. "Top Resilience Tips." July 9. https://instituteofcoaching.org/blogs/top-resilience-tips.

Newby, Alison. 2018. "Mindfulness as a Coaching Tool?" https://coachingfederation.org /blog/mindfulness-coaching-tool.

Waterford.org. 2019. "51 Mindfulness Exercises for Children in the Classroom." www .waterford.org/resources/mindfulnes-activities-for-kids.

CHAPTER 8

Continuing the Journey

Where do I go from here if I don't know where I'm going?

Voices from the Field: Jill

When I launched McFarren Avilés and Associates, I knew what I didn't want to do and where I didn't want to work. I knew that I didn't want to be at a corporate level or so far removed from the direct work with children that I couldn't see the impact of my efforts. I had been working at a management level, far removed from where I felt the real work was happening. The income was steady, and the travel around the world offered the opportunity to meet amazing people, learn about fascinating cultures, and sample delicious food. However, the frustration of working at this ten-thousand-foot level is what finally did me in.

I knew what I didn't want, but I wasn't quite sure what would fill the void. I had the great fortune to have a responsive, reflective coach, Carolyn, who accompanied me on my journey. She took the time to make my voice heard to others and especially to myself. During one of the first meetings we had, Carolyn asked me to prioritize the values that were important to me. Although this exercise seemed interesting and affirming at first, it didn't take on the significance it has today until I felt I was getting in a rut. By going back to those values, I've been able to make meaningful decisions time and again. The other two questions Carolyn asked me were "Where do you want to be in five years?" and "Do you know where you get your energy, from within or from others?" These two questions have contributed to my understanding of what I want to be "when I grow up" and gave me the tools to get there. Since then, I've realized how important it is for me to work with others and create meaningful professional learning

133

opportunities for educators, rekindling relationships with people whom I respect and whose servant leadership inspires me.

Reflective Questions

- Where do you see yourself in five years?

- What tools or resources might support your journey?

- What changes would you like to see in early childhood coaching in general, or are you satisfied with the purposes, resources, strategies, and outcomes it currently achieves for you or your client?

- What support systems can you access that enhance your journey as a coach? Are you part of a community of learners? Do you have someone to bounce ideas off of and who listens when you let off steam?

- How do you recharge your battery? Are there strategies that you would like to share? (Please let us know!)

- Based on what you read in this book, what new ideas could you start using in your practice or advocate to a wider audience?

This chapter focuses on moving forward, taking into account the glacial process of achieving lasting change. It places the culturally responsive coaching process within the current context of coaching initiatives in early childhood. We look at how our role as coaches can be reinforced and contribute to the needed outcomes. We present strategies to keep the momentum going, despite setbacks at an individual, program, or systems level. The key message we want to convey is that the journey of embracing a culturally responsive process is critical to achieving meaningful and sustainable change. We are in this together!

Our first conversation topic builds on the ideas we covered in the previous chapters and conversations through our reflective questions. Coupled together, we are led to the point of asking ourselves, "Now what? Where do I go from here?"

Stages of Change in Our Journey

As with any journey, it helps to know where we are now and where we are going. Some of you are starting out, learning what coaching means to you, what resources are available, and what gifts you bring to the table—the knowledge, skills, and dispositions you offer your clients. There are probably areas where you don't even know what you don't know!

Others are at the stage of learning what you don't know and searching for new information. This is an exciting and overwhelming time. On the one hand, the new knowledge opens doors, leading you on a path to more learning. On the other hand, there is so much information that it's sometimes hard to decipher what is relevant and useful to your clients. As a result of this exploration, you might find yourself back at stage one, not knowing what you don't know until you know it.

A third stage of professional change focuses on incorporating new ideas, knowledge, and perspectives into your work, supporting your client on their professional journey. The adaptations you make to your practice may or may not work, renewing your quest for knowledge. As change is not linear but rather iterative, this process might bring you to search for more information because now you know what you don't know.

The next stage of professional change is associated with a sense of security that you have finally figured out what you want to be when you grow up. It's a stage of focused serenity that comes from stumbling and getting up several times. It's a stage where you have tried new approaches and questioned how they align with your values, beliefs, and practices. This stage also comes with an understanding that we don't always have the answers and that's okay, when in previous stages we might have been afraid to admit our vulnerabilities. With this stage comes the drive to share with others what we know as a way of supporting their journeys. This sharing is not meant to show others what they don't know or prove that you are right and they are wrong. It's a moment of gratitude and paying forward all that you have received from your mentors who had your back all along.

Professional and personal growth is a lifelong process. In whatever stage you find yourself, there are overarching principles that contribute to successfully navigating change and are essential to fulfilling our personal and professional goals. By following them, we are also mirroring the process for our clients. When we have built a strong foundation of our principles, we have this base to fall back on when we face challenges.

Driving Principles That Guide Our Journey

Our first principle is to continuously reflect on what values you have that are nonnegotiable and consider how you know they are being honored. What we value tends to come from our lifelong experiences, and although the way our values manifest may change over time, the values themselves are our constant. For example, one value you may have is *respect*. Respect might look different to you at different stages, but you know when it has been achieved. You might ask yourself, "How do I know when I am respected?" Likewise, "How do I show respect to others?" Understanding what the value of respect looks like will lead you to certain behaviors in a culturally responsive process.

> ### AN EVOLVING UNDERSTANDING OF INFANTS:
> Reflections from an Infant-Toddler Educator
>
> Years ago we showed respect to infants by ensuring they were fed, cared for, and free from harm. Now that I've gone through iterative stages of change, I show respect to infants by asking them, "How can I help you calm down?" and letting them know ahead of time that I will be picking them up to change their diaper. That knowledge was nowhere in my lexicon because I didn't know what I didn't know. I didn't know that an infant's brain is so responsive to every interaction; I didn't know that an infant's sense of self develops when I take the time to respond to their cues. Now I know, and now showing respect to infants is my constant.

Another principle asserts that finding passion in the impact we have on clients is what fuels our professional journey. When we as servant leaders identify how our work is positively influencing the lives of others, it energizes us to continue. This principle is sometimes hard to keep our eyes on when we are responding to the competing priorities that come our way. Completing reports and making sure that our clients are improving on their scores or complying with regulations may make a difference in the short run. However, when we keep in mind how our actions support our clients at a professional and personal level, then our commitment to a culturally responsive coaching process is affirmed. How you respond to your client influences how they feel, which affects how they make the children under their care feel. Completing a predetermined number of coaching sessions is not an end in itself. It's the passion and energy that you bring to the table that makes the difference. It's when you practice being a servant leader and focus on your clients' well-being, autonomy, and competencies that you foster sustainable change.

> ### Reflection
>
> When have you felt passionate about the positive impact that you are having on a client? Have you been reenergized when you see how a client's eyes light up or they change their perspective because of what you said to them?

A third principle is to take care of yourself and embrace a process of lifelong learning. Implementing a culturally responsive coaching process in which we invest a great deal of energy listening to others' voices is draining at times; this holds true whether you are listening to the voice of your client or the organization where you work. There will likely be times when you find that your values and beliefs are challenged or conflict with others'. To continue supporting your clients, you need to find ways to recharge your battery and take care of your well-being. Here are some ways in which we keep refilling our cups.

Continue professional learning

A slew of organizations and events offer opportunities to continue building on our knowledge and skills. It comes down to finding the time and determining which ones you will benefit from the most. A general rule for deciding which opportunities will be the most beneficial is asking the following two questions: what are the people I value offering or participating in, and what questions do I have about methodologies that are out of my comfort zone? For example, while working with a client you might find yourself getting frustrated because you feel they are resistant to change. You may want to search for professional learning opportunities to explore how change happens in others and in yourself. Conversely, engaging in events or reading about strategies that are less aligned with your values offers the opportunity to affirm your practices. For example, perhaps an organization that focuses on compliance and increasing test scores is holding a workshop. As you engage in the event, you can compare it to your own value of sustainable change and become stronger in your conviction that you are on the right path. Such learning also increases your understanding of other approaches so you can identify how your approach is more effective and then articulate this to others.

Look outside the early childhood field to explore how other fields are addressing professional learning and coaching. Some leading resources include the International Coaching Federation (ICF) and the Institute of Coaching–McLean Hospital, a Harvard Medical School affiliate. (You will find links to these organizations at the end of this chapter.)

Network

There is strength in numbers! When we engage with like-minded people, we create synergy. Participating in local or national professional organizations keeps us connected to other professionals and propels the dialogue forward. In addition to the well-recognized national organizations and their local counterparts, such as the National Association for the Education of Young Children (NAEYC) and the National Association for Family Child Care (NAFCC), your local universities feature a wealth of resources, including career placement and research interest groups. Local chapters of the Association for Supervision and Curriculum Development (ASCD) may offer you an opportunity to collaborate with like-minded professionals. Of course, networking opportunities are not limited to professional organizations. Hiking clubs, string quartets, photography clubs, and so many other groups are venues to affirm your environmental, cultural, and artistic values.

Share knowledge and experience at conferences or by mentoring others

You have something important to say that will be meaningful to others. Speaking at conferences and mentoring others affirms you and your work while increasing the impact you have on others' lives, especially children and families. Your work with your clients may seem obvious and nothing extraordinary, but you could be a gift to others who don't yet know what they don't know. We have been surprised when we have found that strategies that we consider essential, such as listening to clients and building a trusting relationship, aren't practiced by others. You have probably encountered moments when you were surprised by how much you knew that others didn't! Share your knowledge and experience, no matter how insignificant or mundane it might feel to you.

Parting Thoughts

We hope that the conversations we brought you into throughout the book have given you a lot of food for thought and answered some questions. However, most important, we hope that the book has affirmed your practices, inspiring you to explore and reflect on your journey and that of your clients. Whether you are a coach, supervisor, education specialist, or anyone else who is involved in supporting adult learners, we hope that the information, strategies, and reflective questions here have infused your practices with the belief that we *all* learn best through trusting relationships. To achieve sustainable change, we need to be servant leaders and mirror the same in others.

> ### Reflection
> What are your go-to resources? Are they aligned with your values, beliefs, and practices?

Revisit the questions on page 134. How have your responses changed? How have they stayed the same?

Competencies

- Be a reflective learner.

- Align your values with your practice and understand that what they look like may evolve over time.

Practices

- Continue with your professional learning.

- Participate and contribute to networks.

- Share your knowledge.

- Be kind to yourself.

- Invest in a personal coach.

Hear Your Client's Voice

- How does your client influence your drive?

- What can your client learn from you about knowing where to go and how to get there?

Hear Your Voice

- What information in this chapter resonates the most for you?

- How can you continue your professional journey?

- What support mechanisms do you need to refill your cup?

References and Resources

Association for Supervision and Curriculum Development (ASCD). www.ascd.org /Default.aspx.

Institute of Coaching. https://instituteofcoaching.org.

International Coaching Federation (ICF). https://coachfederation.org.

Stanier, Michael Bungay. 2020. *The Advice Trap: Be Humble, Stay Curious & Change the Way You Lead Forever*. Page Two Books.

Washington State Department of Children, Youth and Families. 2019. "Relationship-Based Standards of Professional Development." www.dcyf.wa.gov/sites/default/files /pdf/RBPDStandards.pdf.

———. n.d. "Professional Development Strategies." www.dcyf.wa.gov/services /earlylearning-profdev/professional-development-strategies.

Index

coaches and coaching
    client's earlier professional experiences with,
        51–52
    data and quantification of outcomes, xviii
    effect of own filters on, 20–21
    goals of, 45
    intentionality and, 13–14, 15
    language and ability to communicate with
        clients, 68–69
    strength-based, 13
    transactional approach to, 8–9
    See also culturally responsive coaches and
        coaching
Coaching with the Brain in Mind (Rock and Page),
    17
colleagues
    importance of having trusted, 33
    reflective questions, 33
comfort zone, identifying and moving beyond,
    24
    communication
        with families, 64
        language differences and, 68–69
continuity of care, 76
COVID-19, 40, 75
culturally responsive coaches and coaching
    as agents of change, 88–89, 91–93
    antidiscrimination and, 12
    awareness of own culture, 51
    building resilience
        connecting with self and others, 131
        fostering self-care and compassion, 128–129
        listening to understand, 128
        principles for, 126
        reframing mindset, 130
        self-trust and vulnerability, 126–127
        through problem solving, 129
    data collection, 101–103, 111, 114
    data use by, 101–103
    discrimination and, 11
    equity and
        finding resources to meet needs of every
            family, 88–89
        strategies to support, 89–93
        understanding client's actual needs, 11, 83–84,
            85
        understanding own culture, 83
    goal of, xix
    goals of organization hiring, 53–54
    knowing goals of clients, 47
    learning from mistakes, 10
    own biases, 89
    practices, 14–15, 41

reflection by clients and, 52
reflective questions, 36, 77, 83
relationships with clients
    building, 34, 35, 44
    client-centeredness of coaches, 46–47, 124
    coach's knowledge of background and culture
        of, 7–8, 81–83
    culturally responsive coaching approach and,
        9–10, 124
    first contact with, 34
    gathering information and being alone in FCC
        settings, 70–71
    language and ability of coaches to
        communicate, 68–69
    listening with empathy, 55
    messages transmitted by coaches to, 34
    reflective questions, 45
    understanding actual needs of, 11, 55, 83–84,
        85
    self-reflection as foundation of, 18
    as servant leaders, 35
    as transformational coaching tool, 9–11
    unique populations, 73–74
cultural responsiveness
    of client, 56
    data collection systems and, 103–109
    described, 5
    dominant culture and, 86–87
    elements of, 6–7
    strategies for increasing, 56
    use of data, 101–103
culture
    biases and assumptions and, 89
    changing nature of, 84
    of client, 49–50, 90
    coaches' awareness of own, 51
    cultural responsiveness and dominant, 86–87
    data collection tools and, 109
    finding balance between science and, 8
    formation of, 4
    importance of understanding client's, 7–8
    influence of, 2, 4, 5
        on assessment, 99
        on behaviors, 19, 25
        on biases and assumptions, 51
        on body language, 25, 46
        expectations of children, 27, 52–53, 76
        individual's response to adversity, 125
        on program setting's, 64
        on values, 26
    injustices arising from competing, 84
    mistakes and, 125, 128
    as reflection of individuals, 4

Freire, Paulo, 81
funding, requirements for, xi

G

genetic makeup and learning, 27
goals
    of clients, 45, 47, 53–54, 85
    of culturally responsive coaches and coaching,
        xix, 53–54
    dominant culture and, 86
    values' connection to, 54
growth. *See* change

H

Harvard Education Implicit Association Test (IAT),
    39
heritage. *See* culture
Hooks, Bell, 1

I

India, 1–2
in-home program settings
    family, friend, and neighbor, 66–67
    family child care, 67–71
    inner voice, learning to listen to, 21–22
intentionality
    being present in the moment and, 13
    coaching and, 13–14, 15
    culture and, 4
interventions, data and quantification of outcomes,
    xviii

K

Kuhn, Thomas, 5

L

language
    ability of coaches to communicate with clients,
        68–69
    perspective and, 65
leaders and leadership
    characteristics, 11
    coaches and early childhood educators as, 35
    passion of, 136–137
    reflective questions, 36
learning
    as adult, 27
    continuing professional, 137–139
    daily routines and, 76
    influences on, 26–27
    mistakes and failures as opportunity for, 10, 28,
        125

open-ended compared to closed-ended
    questions, 27–28
reflective questions, 28, 76

M

McFarren Avilés & Associates, xxiv
memories, 48
mentoring, 138–139
mindfulness, practice of, 31, 129
mindset, reframing, 130
mistakes
    culture and, 125, 128
    learning from, 10, 28, 125
    reflecting on, 28
    resilience and, xxiii
    vulnerability and, 30
motivation
    identifying own, 23–25
    reflective questions, 25

N

networking and change, 138
nomenclature and perspective, 65

P

Page, Linda J., 17
pairwise ranking of data, 112–113
parallel talk, 35
Participatory Learning and Action (PLA) data
        collection process
    basic facts about, 110, 111
    culturally responsive coaching and, 114
    pairwise ranking, 112–113
positive, focusing on the, 13, 55–56
positive deviance (PD) data collection process
    basic facts about, 110
    culturally responsive coaching and, 111
prioritization, 129
problem solving, 129
professional organizations, 138
program settings
    connections to fellow professionals, 61
    influence of culture and, 64
    in-home
        center-based, 71–73
        family, friend, and neighbor, 66–67
        family child care, 67–71
    keeping children at forefront, 63–64
    reflective questions, 62, 64
    responsiveness of environment and, 69–70